GUITAR ROOKIE TO ROCKSTAR - BOOK 1

GUITAR ROOKIE TO ROCKSTAR - BOOK 1

A STEP-BY-STEP ABSOLUTE BEGINNER'S GUIDE TO CHORDS, STRUMMING & PLAYING YOUR FIRST 3 SONGS IN JUST 14 DAYS

IAN DAVIES

PAUL STERLING

First Note™
Beginner to Boss

ISBN13: 978-93-47026-85-0 (Ebook Edition)
ISBN13: 978-93-47026-16-4 (Paperback Edition)
ISBN13: 978-93-47026-99-7 (Hardcover Edition)

DEDICATION

To all the brave beginners picking up a guitar for the very first time - welcome to the tribe. May your strings stay in tune, your fingers toughen quickly, and your excitement never fade. Here's to the first chord of an unforgettable journey.

CLAIM YOUR FREE BONUSES!

THANKS FOR PICKING UP GUITAR ROOKIE TO ROCKSTAR BOOK 1! TO HELP YOU GET EVEN FASTER RESULTS, WE'VE INCLUDED A FEW EXCLUSIVE BONUSES - 100% FREE.

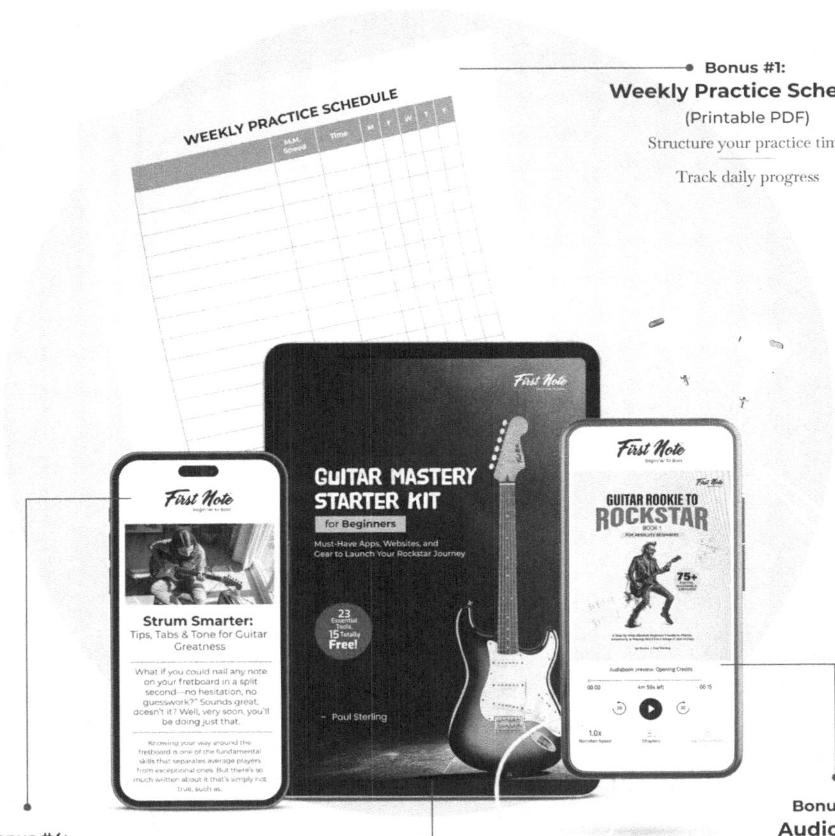

Bonus #1:
Weekly Practice Schedule
(Printable PDF)
Structure your practice time
Track daily progress

Bonus #2:
Audio Files
Hear every exercise played correctly
Practice by ear and improve faster

Bonus #3:
Guitar Mastery Starter Kit
(Printable PDF)
Must-have apps, tools & resources
Beginner gear tips
Practice strategies that work

Bonus #4:
FirstNote Newsletter
Monthly tips, lessons & updates
Early access to new books & offers

Download everything at

playfirstnote.com/bonuses

CONTENTS

INTRODUCTION

YOU'RE ABOUT TO START ONE OF THE MOST EXCITING JOURNEYS OF YOUR LIFE

Over the next 14 days, the first book in our exciting step-by-step guides to guitar mastery - Guitar Rookie to Rockstar - will set you on the right path to becoming a great guitarist.

In just two short weeks, you will master all the basics, including the...

- Names and functions of every part of your guitar
- How to hold a pick and strum properly
- How to tune a guitar with a tuner, an app, and by ear
- The five most important root chords for beginners
- Plus, you'll learn how to play three complete songs, including the chords, rhythm patterns, and melodies!

But before we get to all that, I have some good news and some bad news, which would you like first? Since most people prefer to start with the bad news, let's go with that…

According to Fender, your chances of success are very low

Yes, I'm sorry to start on such a downer, but according to a survey that guitar giant Fender (creator of some of the most iconic guitars and amplifiers in history, such as the Fender Stratocaster and Fender Telecaster) conducted between between May 8th and June 13th, 2021, 90% of all people who start playing the guitar give up within the first 12 months, with the majority stopping within three months!

This is a shocking figure; basically, only one in ten people who decide to learn the instrument are still playing it a year later.

Now that's sunk in, it's time for the good news…

According to me, your chances of success are virtually guaranteed

I have been teaching for decades, and from my experience with the hundreds, if not thousands, of people I have taught over that time, very few of them give up. I would say fewer than 5%, with the majority continuing to play for many years, and many turning it into successful careers.

So, what's the difference? Well, since the dawn of the internet, it has never been easier to gather information on any subject you are interested in, including learning the guitar. There are endless videos showing you how to play just about anything or any song on YouTube, as well as loads of sites that contain TABS or explain how certain techniques are played - whatever you want to know, it's out there, with a simple search.

But there are a few downsides to having instant access to all this info, especially when you are just starting out. The most frustrating for beginners is knowing what they should learn, in what order, and whether they are learning it from someone who actually knows what they are talking about.

This is why I think the results of Fender's survey paint such a negative picture. You want to learn to play, and there are endless resources on the internet, so why not teach yourself? Excellent, you know what your favorite songs are, so you do a quick YouTube search and have a go at playing them.

But your fingers can't stretch that far, and when you pick or strum the notes, it doesn't sound anything like the song or what they are playing in the video. No problem, let's try another song, that must be easier, but it isn't, it still sounds terrible when you try and play it. You thought learning to play would be far easier than this, and you lose confidence; however hard you try, it just sounds terrible.

The problem is that you are learning songs that are far too difficult for you to play at this stage of your development. They might well be easy in four or five months, after you've learned easier songs and the correct techniques, but for now, basically impossible. So, you give up!

If, however, someone guides you through exactly what you need to learn in the correct order to be able to play these songs, you simply follow the path and easily achieve the results you are looking for in a few months time. I will be your guide, ensuring that you quickly improve through each step to become the guitarist you have always dreamt of being.

Knowing what to learn is the key to becoming a great guitarist; without that roadmap, it is very difficult to continuously improve your skills. This is why I think 90% of those who try to play give up. But luckily, thanks to this series of books, you won't be one of them; you will be one of the 95% of guitarists who succeed!

But how can I guarantee your Success?

To be honest, I can't, but from experience, I know that if you carefully go through and absorb the information and practice each step of this guide, you will become a guitarist.

How good you will be will be down to your goals and ambition. If you only want to strum simple songs and have a sing-along around a campfire with friends, no problem at all, you'll learn everything you need to be able to do that. Or if you want to jam with some friends, that will also be covered. Even if you want to form a band and go for the big time, everything you need to know is included.

I will take you from an absolute beginner, step by step, through every technique you need to know to play the songs you love. We will be focusing on having fun and teaching things that you actually want to play, not endless boring exercises and yawn-inducing music theory that will put you to sleep faster than Christmas dinner with all the trimmings.

So, let's get straight to it and start the most exciting musical journey of your life!

CHAPTER 1
BREAKING DOWN THE INSTRUMENT
PARTS OF THE GUITAR AND HOW TO HANDLE IT

It's time to get going… excited? You should be, this is going to be a fun ride.

As with any practical skill, there is quite a lot to explain before we get to the nitty-gritty of guitar playing, so hang on in there as we go over the basics. These fundamentals are important, so make sure you understand them before moving forward.

Let's start by getting to know the…

PARTS OF THE GUITAR

Before we learn how to play the fantastic piece of wood with strings on it that's in your lap, you'll need to know the names of the various bits. You'll also need to know how to hold it properly, as well as how to hold that small, awkward-looking piece of plastic we call a pick.

The guitar can be divided into three main parts: the body, the neck, and the headstock. These will be the same regardless of the type of guitar you own - electric, acoustic, or classical.

The Body

The body is the large section that rests on your lap. It is the part of the instrument that produces its sound. For an acoustic or classical guitar, the sound is created by the strings vibrating, which are then amplified and projected outward by the body. In the case of electric guitars, the vibrations of the strings are captured by a pickup that then sends the signal to be amplified externally so that we can hear it.

The Neck

Coming out of one side of the body, you will find a long stick-like piece of wood; this is the neck. This is where you will be placing your fretting hand to press down on the strings. It has lots of thin strips of metal running across it; these are the frets. Placing your fingers between these creates different notes.

The Headstock

This is positioned at the end of the neck, and its main purpose is to hold six small mechanical parts - the 'tuning heads', which are used to tune the instrument. These are also known as 'tuners', 'tuning pegs', 'tuning machines', or 'machine heads'.

When you play a string, either with a finger or using a pick, it will produce a sound, which is called a 'note'. Each open string needs to be a particular note at a certain pitch to be 'in-tune', i.e., sound the way the guitar should sound.

If the note is not correct, you need to turn the string's tuning head to either raise or lower the tension. This will result in an increase or decrease of pitch, which is how the instrument is tuned.

I know that all sounds a bit complicated, but don't worry, I'll be going through it in far more detail very soon.

Note: The three parts of the guitar are the same on both right and left-handed instruments, but the neck goes in the opposite direction for left-handed guitars.

To avoid any confusion, I will use the term ***fretting hand*** for all references to the hand you use to play the notes on the neck and the term ***picking hand*** for the one you use to play or strum the strings throughout this book.

The photographs below show all three sections as well as the names of the other key parts:

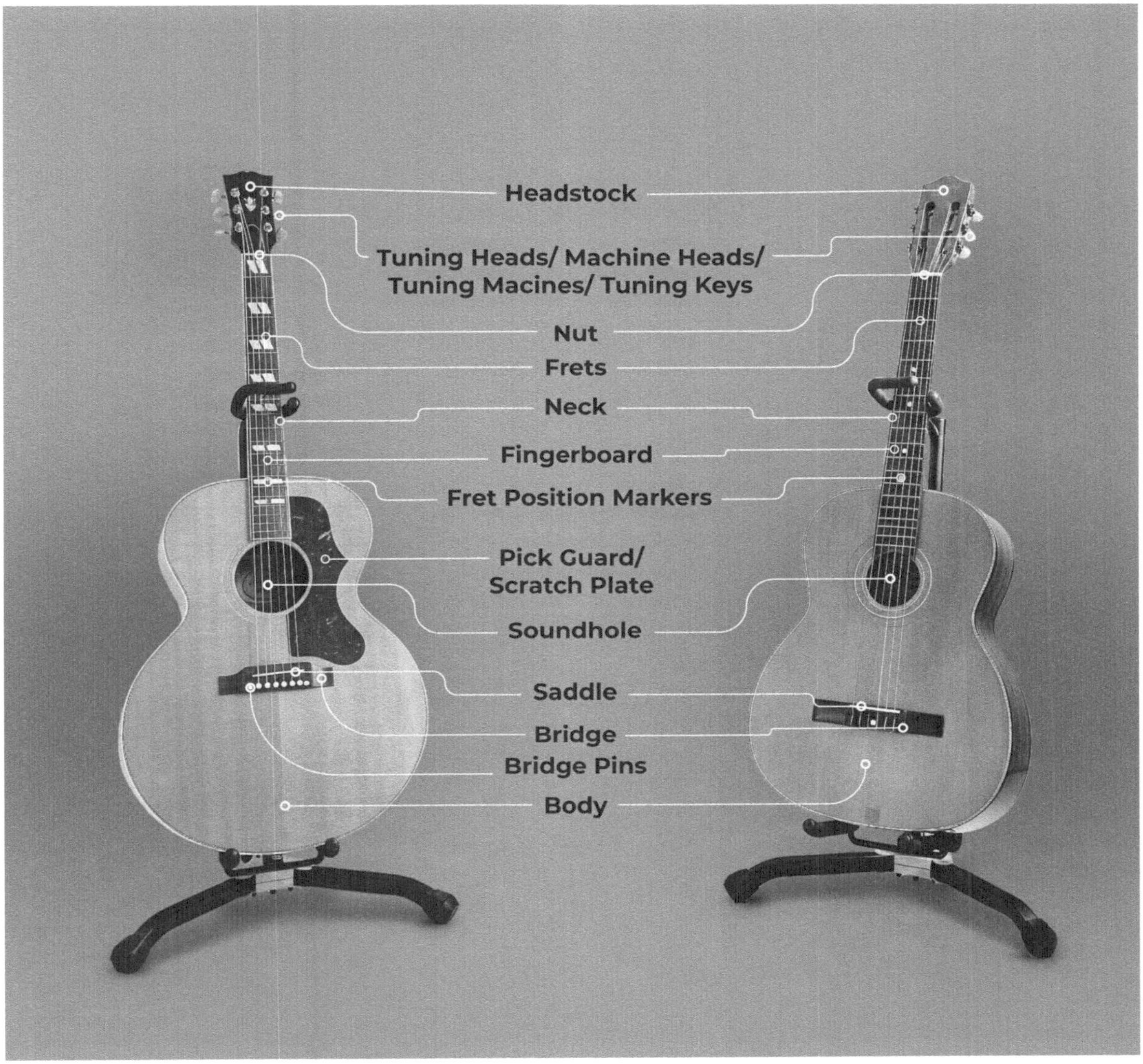

Pic 1 - The parts of an Acoustic and a Classical Guitar

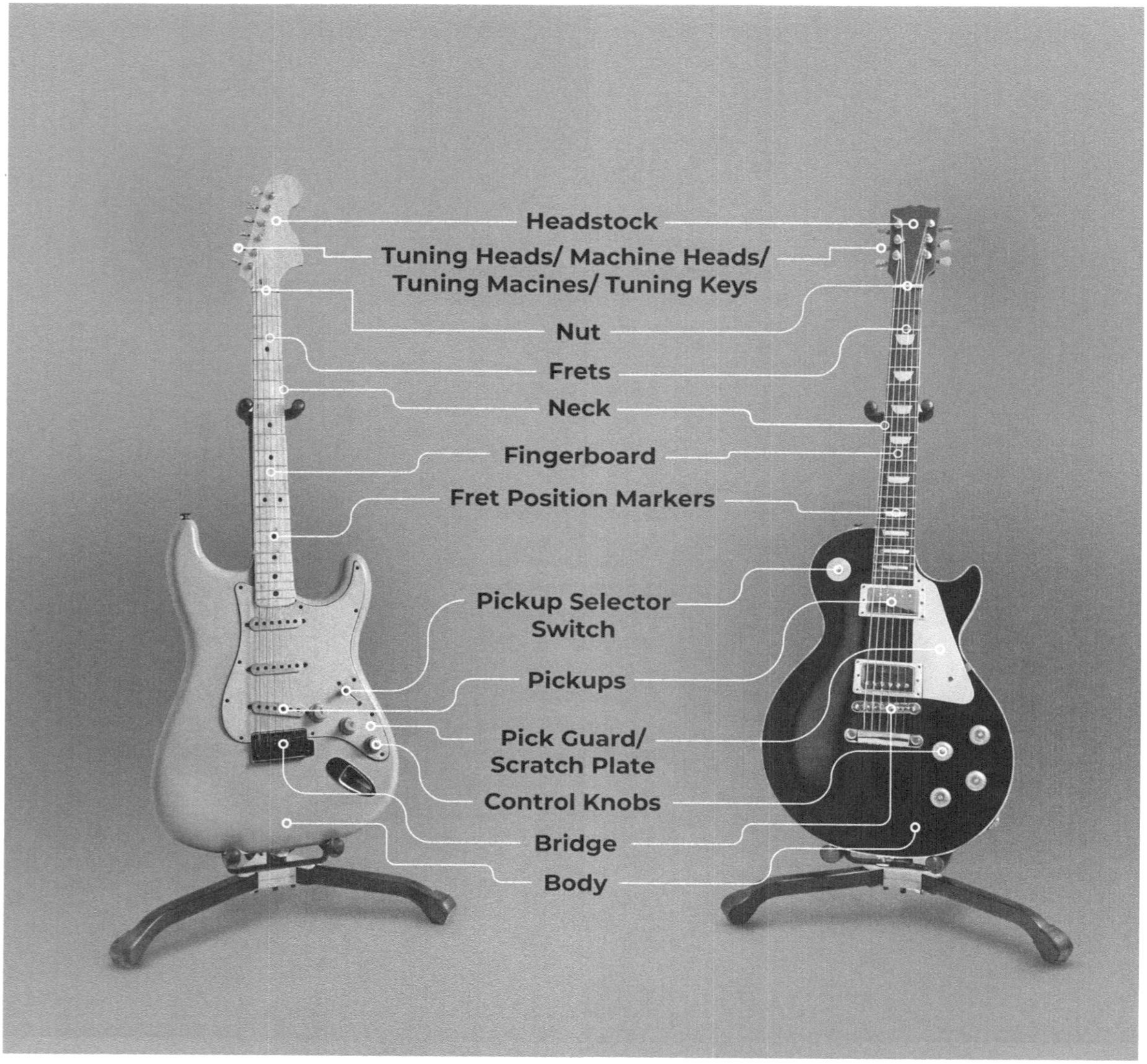

Pic 2 - The parts of Electric Guitars

Now that you know what every part is called, let's move on to…

HOW TO HOLD A GUITAR

Even though Jimmy Page and Slash look fantastic with a guitar hanging below their waist, they didn't play like that on day one. So find yourself a comfortable place to sit, preferably on an office chair with adjustable height that doesn't have any arms on it. If it does have arms, get yourself some Allen keys and take them off; you can put them back on when you reach guitar ninja status.

Make sure that your back is straight and that you are not slouching; this is why a height-adjustable office chair is invaluable. Learning to play on a sofa or a reclining chair is very comfortable, but it can put pressure on your back and shoulders, which can become painful, as well as limit the movement of your arms, wrists, and hands, so spend the time to find a suitable chair to practice - your body will thank you for it.

Place the guitar on your lap, with the arch of the lower body resting on your right leg (left leg for left-handed players). It feels a bit weird, doesn't it? Not exactly comfortable. This is normal for most beginners, but don't worry, it will feel much more natural in a few days and fit like a glove after a few weeks.

Note: Classical guitarists usually place the guitar on the other leg and use a footstand to raise the leg slightly. However, unless you specifically want to learn classical guitar technique, play whatever guitar you have on the right leg (or left for southpaws).

Now that the guitar is in position, your picking hand should be above the sound hole (on acoustic guitars) or between the pickups (on electrics), with your fretting hand supporting the neck, as shown below:

Pic 3 - Perfect playing position

The height of the neck is very important and will vary slightly from one person to the next, depending on what they find most comfortable, particularly for the wrist of the fretting hand. You need to experiment with this until you find what works for you.

The wrist of your fretting hand needs to be relaxed with all four fingers pointing upward and inward onto the fretboard. Your thumb should also be pointing straight up and positioned halfway between your first and fourth fingers on the fretboard, but on the back of the neck, as shown below:

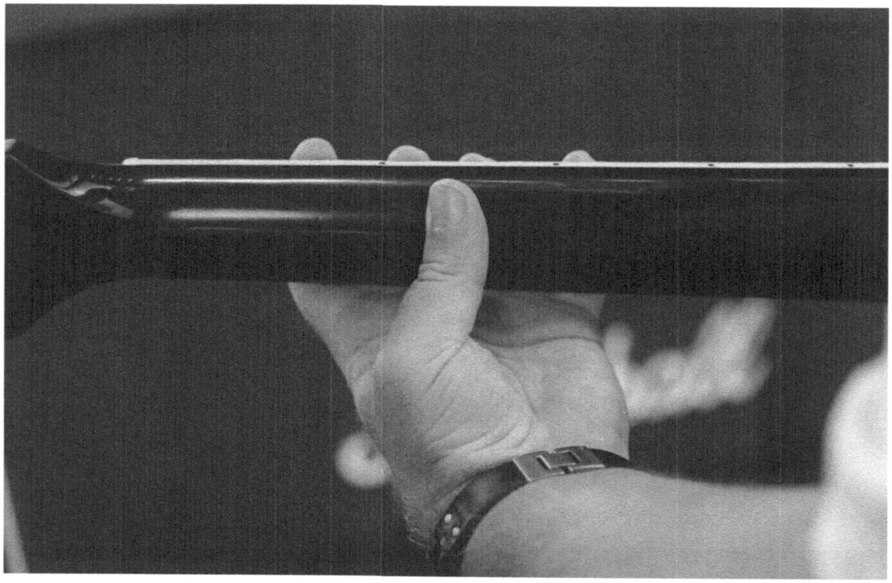

Pic 4 - Thumb is positioned at 90 degrees to the neck

Even though it is more comfortable, avoid hooking your thumb over the neck; this will make playing chords correctly much more difficult.

I know that you've seen all your favorite guitarists do it - it is, as I said, the most comfortable way to play - but they only do it when they know they can. When they need to play more difficult chord positions, they will make adjustments, and you won't see their thumbs hanging over the top of the neck.

Pic 5 - How not to play, even though your heroes do!

Finally, make sure that the bottom of your guitar is flat on your lap; don't be tempted to have it at an angle so that it is easier to see where your fingers are and what strings you are picking.

Most beginners do this because they have no confidence in where their fingers will end up, but make sure that you don't fall into this trap; it will really hold you back as your skills develop.

If you need to check the position of a certain finger in a chord and can't see it clearly, adjust the position of the guitar, but put it back flat on your lap afterwards before you continue playing.

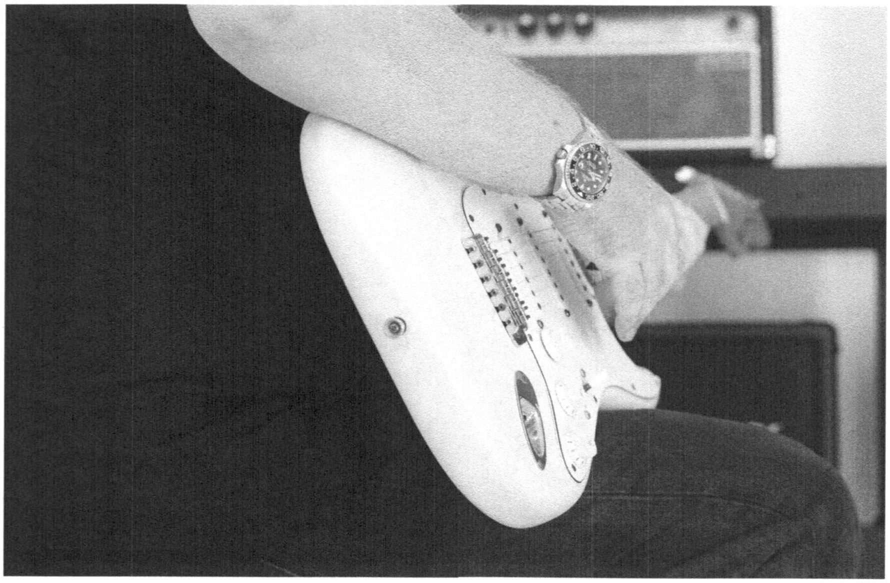

Pic 6 - Guitar correctly placed flat on the lap

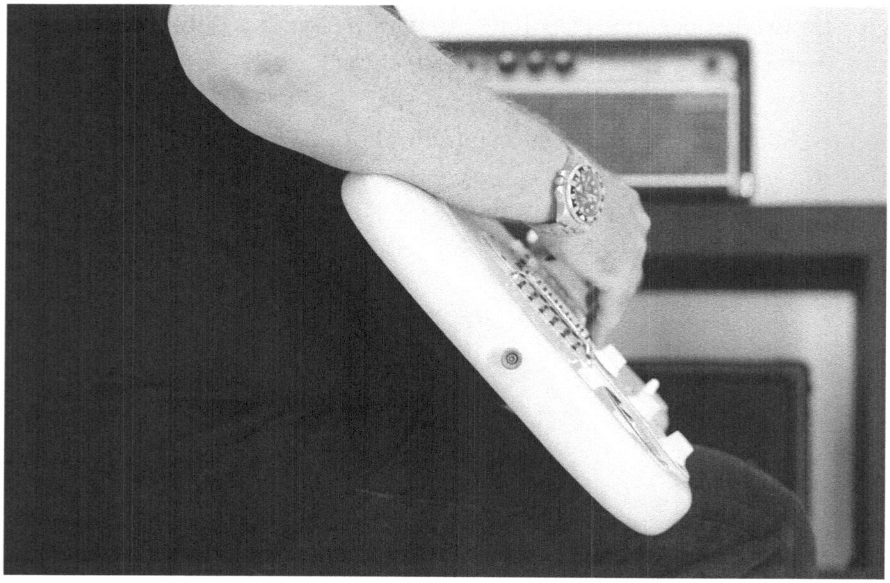

Pic 7 - Guitar at an angle, bad technique

In the Pic 6, the player's arm and wrist are flat and relaxed, ready to play whatever comes next. In the Pic 7, the angle of the guitar is forcing the player to awkwardly bend their arm and wrist, making it harder and more uncomfortable to play.

Should I Sit, or should I… Stand?

Learning to play standing up is difficult enough, even after you have learnt to play sitting down. Even a quite accomplished player, while sat in a chair, will take at least a few weeks (or longer) to get to the same level while standing up. Therefore, playing standing up at this stage is just putting additional stress on your body for no gain.

So, forget about standing for now. I know that playing sitting down isn't as cool, but as a beginner, you need to be working on remembering information and perfecting your technique. This is much easier to do while sitting down than standing up.

Your time to stand and strut your stuff will come soon enough. For now, concentrate on becoming as good a guitarist as you can; there will be plenty of time to run around the stage and show off your skills to an admiring audience in the future.

HOW TO HOLD A GUITAR PICK

Guitar picks, or plectrums, are usually small pieces of plastic that are used to strike the strings.

They are manufactured from various materials, including plastics such as celluloid, nylon, acrylic, or Delrin (a synthetic thermoplastic polymer), as well as various metals, or even glass, bone, or carbon fiber.

Plastic picks are by far the most common and the best option for beginners. They come in different shapes, sizes, textures, and thicknesses. I recommend the standard shape, as shown below, and a medium thickness for most beginners.

If you have a heavy hand, then you can go for a thinner pick until you get it under control, but most beginners manage to play happily with a medium pick. Avoid heavy/thick picks; these are best for playing lead guitar, which we will be moving onto, but not in this book.

Pic 8 - Standard guitar picks

Once you are comfortable using your pick, which should only take a few weeks, you can experiment with other sizes, textures, and materials. You can even buy mixed sets that contain different sizes so that you can find the one you are most comfortable with.

This isn't vitally important at this early stage, but as you improve, you will find that certain picks are more comfortable than others and become your favorites.

How Many Fingers?

Every guitarist holds their pick differently; there are guidelines, of course, but how one guitarist holds a pick will differ slightly from the next. Therefore, you need to find what is most comfortable for you.

The first decision is how many fingers. I recommend using your thumb and one finger to hold your pick, but lots of guitarists use their thumb and two fingers.

I prefer using my thumb and one finger because I find that it makes pick movements more agile, allowing me to move the pick in very subtle ways. However, if you find two fingers more comfortable, go for it.

The other advantage of using your thumb and one finger is that hybrid picking (using a pick and one, two, or three of your fingers to fingerpick at the same time) will be easier in the future if you decide to learn the technique.

Where should the tip of the pick be pointing?

There is much more agreement on this, with nearly every guitarist having the tip of the pick pointing in the same direction as the tip of their first finger, which is positioned at 90 degrees to the thumb.

This ensures that the pick is in the optimum position, i.e., pointing straight at the soundhole on acoustic guitars, to strike the strings evenly as you strum either downward or upward, or pick a string.

Pic 9 - How to hold a pick correctly

And here is how not to hold a pick: the first picture shows the pick being held too far to the left, the second, too far to the right…

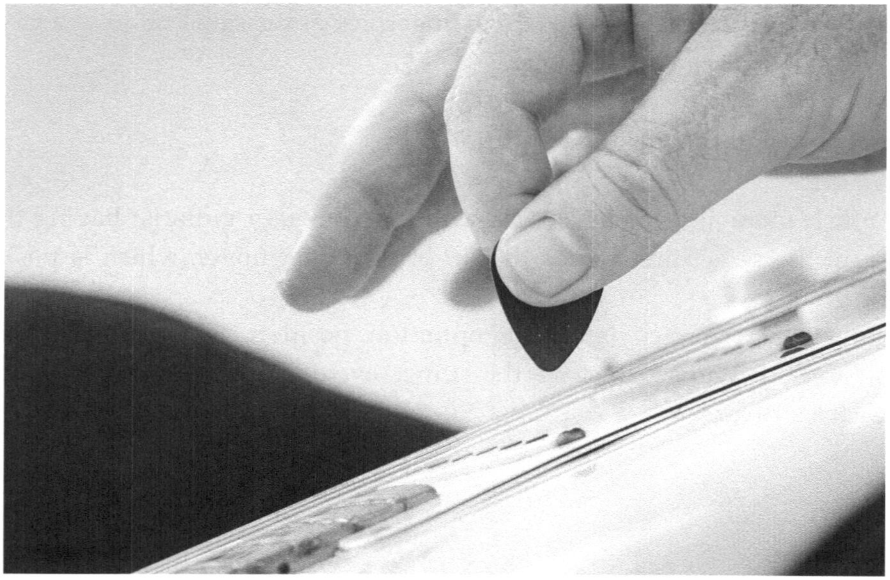

Pic 10 - The tip of the pick is too far to the right

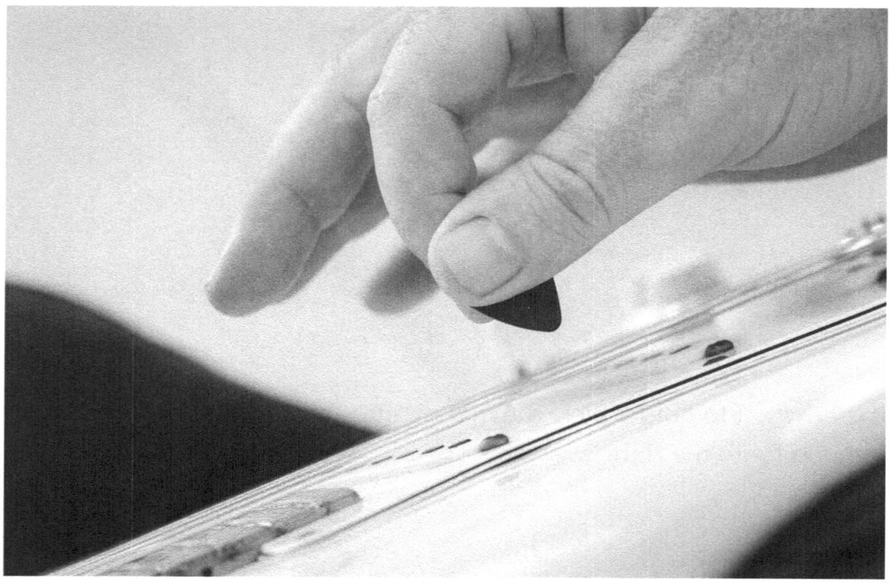

Pic 11 - Now it is too far to the left

A QUICK GUIDE TO STRUMMING

Now that you have your trusty pick in hand, I know that you are itching to strum the guitar to hear the wonderful sound it makes.

Strum by moving your arm in a downward motion from near the top of the body, across the strings, ending near the edge of the bottom half of the body. That's right, the arc of the strum is a lot wider than most beginners think. To create the right sound, you need to strum in a much wider arc than simply starting at the thick strings and finishing at the thin strings.

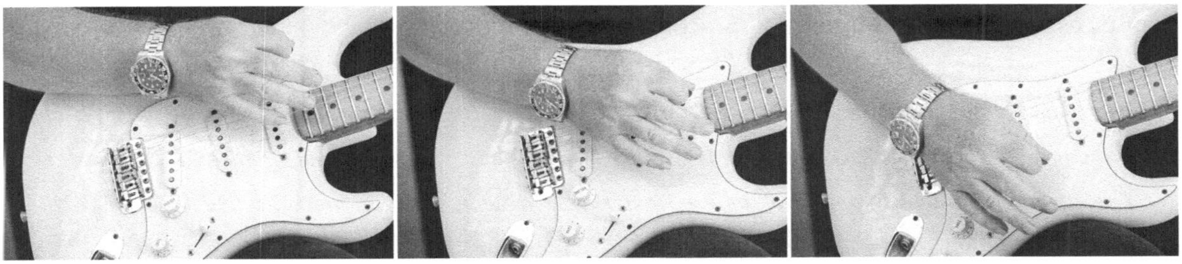

Pics 12, 13, & 14 - The start, middle and end of the strumming arc

Or, from a slightly different angle…

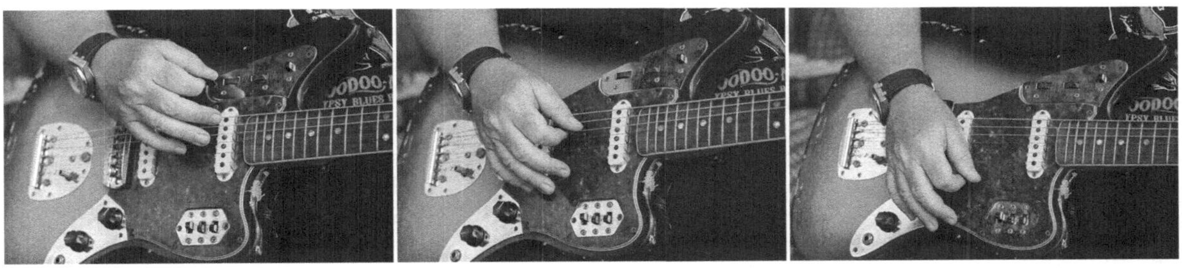

Pics 15, 16, & 17 - The full strumming arc

Keep your wrist flexible throughout and try to strum so gently that the motion is not compromised as you come into contact with the strings.

And that, in a nutshell, is how to strum, so grab your guitar and give it a go. It probably won't sound great at this stage because you will be hitting the strings too hard. Remember that being gentle is the key; when you've mastered the technique, you can rock out and hit the strings a lot harder and still get a great sound.

You should now have the guitar sat semi-comfortably on your lap, with your pick in hand and be ready for the practical aspects of learning to play, but before we can get to that, there is one final, but ever so important, thing to cover…

HOW TO TUNE A GUITAR

As the old saying goes…

You can tune a guitar, but you can't tuna fish

Or something like that? Can't quite remember, to be honest, anyway… There are two ways to tune your guitar: either using technology to give you a helping hand by using a Tuner or a Tuning App, or doing it by ear. The electronic method is a lot easier and produces far better results, especially for beginners, so I recommend it at this early stage.

Pro Tip: Don't become reliant on this method of tuning. Tuning by ear is a rite of passage for every guitarist, and there are numerous reasons why you need to master the skill, the most important being how much it will improve your ability to recognize and distinguish notes, i.e., ear training.

As for tuna fish, I'll leave you to enjoy them any way you like. And while you do, here's some info on…

Tuning with a Tuner or an App

Tuners are normally small boxes filled with electronics that do all the heavy lifting when it comes to getting your guitar perfectly in tune. They can be standalone, or you can get clip-on versions that attach to the headstock. Depending on the tuner, they may either detect string vibrations or you need to plug a cable into them from an electric or electro-acoustic guitar, or usually, both.

They are incredibly simple to use - turn them on, play a string, and your tuning buddy will tell you what note it is and whether it is flat or sharp. If it is flat, it means that it is lower in pitch than it should be, and you need to turn the tuning head that corresponds with that string to increase the tension on the string and therefore sharpen it to get it in tune.

If it is sharp, it is higher in pitch than it should be, and you need to lower the tension on the string by turning the tuning head once again.

The direction you need to turn the tuning head will depend on the design of your guitar and the layout of your headstock. The thickest string, which is called the 'Low E', is normally tuned by turning the tuning head counter-clockwise, but there are exceptions. Start by turning it counter-clockwise; if the string goes up in pitch, i.e., increases in tension, you are making the note sharper, if it goes down in pitch, flatter.

Tuning apps work in exactly the same way as physical tuners, but are on your smartphone.

They are widely available from wherever you get your apps, work well, and are usually free for the basic versions.

Pic 18 - BOSS Tuner App

Apps are fantastic for beginners, but I recommend getting a physical tuner later on your journey because I find them to be slightly more accurate due to the bigger and better displays. You can also plug electric guitars directly into them with a cable, therefore eliminating the microphone, which can pick up any sound, not only the note you are playing.

What pitches should the notes be?

Most guitarists play, and most songs are written, in standard tuning. However, this can vary, but for the purpose of this book, that is all we will be covering. It features the following notes:

6th String (the Thickest) - E
5th String - A
4th String - D
3rd String - G
2nd String - B
1st String (the thinnest) - E

Note: Even though it might seem strange, the strings are counted from the thinnest to the thickest, i.e., the thinnest is the 1st string, while the thickest is the 6th. This may seem counterintuitive, but it's something that you will quickly get used to.

You've probably noticed that there are two E notes, one for the thickest string - the Low E - and one for the thinnest - the high e. These notes sound the same but are two octaves apart. Don't worry about what an octave is for now; we'll be looking at them soon. As I mentioned, I won't be filling your head with boring music theory until it is necessary.

These notes are the six strings of the guitar when you play them open, i.e., you don't put a finger on a string that changes its pitch. And you'll need to remember them, or you won't know what note each string needs to be when you tune it. The easiest way to do this is with a quirky mnemonic, such as...

Elephants Always Destroy Guitars Before Eating
Eddie Ate Dynamite, Good Bye Eddie
Elephants And Donkeys Grow Big Ears
Eat All Day, Get Big Easy

Take your pick, or better still, make one up about a friend or family member and something amusing or unusual that happened to them.

Your first Exercise and an Introduction to TAB

Let's now take a look at your first exercise to make sure that you remember the names of the open strings. To do this, we will be using TAB, a simplified way of writing music for fretted instruments.

You'll notice that the 'TAB' diagram below has six lines on it; these represent the six strings of the guitar.

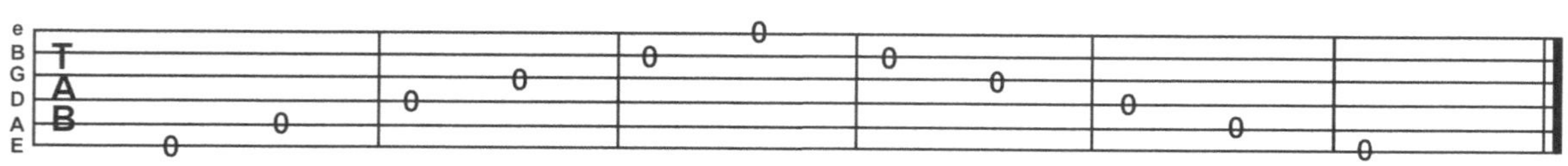

The line at the bottom of the diagram is the Low E string, the thickest string, because that is closest to you when you are playing and looking down on the guitar. The top line is the high e string, the thinnest string, because it is furthest away from you when you are playing, as shown below...

Pic 19 - Guitar headstock turned upside down showing the names of the strings matching the TAB

Seems strange, I know, but this is the most logical method of displaying the information and will become second nature very quickly. The number '0' means that you need to play an open string. Here's the TAB again…

Exercise 1

Note: the top section of the diagram is standard music notation; this is only there for reference, you don't need to worry about it at this stage.

It's now time to play the first six notes, start with the open Low E string, and say its name out loud as you play it. Then play the A, the D, the G, the B, and finally the high e string, remembering to say every note as you play it. This will help you quickly remember the string names, so don't be shy, say the note out loud, and be proud of it.

Now go back down the strings, playing the B string through to the Low E string. Repeat the exercise five more times or until you are comfortable playing and naming all the notes.

To download the audio files for the exercises mentioned in this section, head to **playfirstnote.com/bonuses.**

Let's get the guitar in Tune

It's now time to turn on your tuner or get your smartphone and open your tuning app. Play the thickest string, which you now know is the Low E string, and see what your tuner or app says the note is.

If it is an E, excellent, but this is highly unlikely. If the note is lower in pitch than an E (such as a C, C#, D, or D# - the notes work alphabetically), turn the tuning head (usually counter-clockwise) until the tuner or app says that the note is an E. This is usually also accompanied by a sound and/or flashing lights to signify that the note is in tune. If you go too far and the note becomes sharp, reverse the process.

If the open note is sharper than an E (such as an F, F#, G, or G#), turn the tuning head (usually clockwise) until the tuner or app indicates that the note is an E with the accompanying sound and/or flashing lights.

Top Tip and a Word of Caution: It takes beginners a while to realize how taut the strings on a guitar should be. If a string seems very tight and the tuner or app is still telling you to make it sharper, you have more than likely missed the note - if you carry on tightening the string, it will break.

The best thing to do is to lower the tension on the string until you reach the target note. If the string is still quite taut, then it is at the correct pitch; if it is very loose, then you need to sharpen it again slowly until you reach the correct pitch for the string.

Perfection

It's very important to get each note as precisely in tune as possible; therefore, try and get the needle of your tuner, or the 'needle' in the app's display, to be dead center.

If a string is slightly out, you probably won't hear the difference yet, but over time, your ear will get used to hearing notes that are not perfectly in tune, making it harder to tell if notes are correct in the future.

So, start as you mean to go on, with every string perfectly in tune before you begin every practice session.

Tuning by Ear

We all love our apps, our smartphone is always with us, so why bother spending the time and effort to learn to tune the guitar by ear?

Well, imagine you're having fun around the campfire at a fantastic beach party with all your friends, and they are passing around a guitar because everyone wants a sing-along?

Fantastic, you know how to play, you take hold of the guitar and get ready to impress the socks off everyone - even though they aren't wearing any, it's a beach party after all! Anyway, back to the plot…

You give the guitar a strum and… Oh, No! It's out of tune, and your phone is out of battery. You could ask to borrow a phone, but it won't have a tuning app on it… you're screwed!!!

If only you'd listened to your old guitar teacher and learned how to tune the guitar by ear, you would now be the beach party superstar and have admiring glances from everyone around you.

So, let's get straight to it…

In a perfect world, you start by tuning the low E string to a reference pitch - such as a piano, a tuning fork, a pitch on an app or the internet, or a song. This is to make sure that you are in standard tuning.

However, if you don't have a reference pitch, you can still tune the guitar, but it will be 'tuned to itself'. It will sound perfectly in tune, but if you jam with a friend or try to play along with a song on YouTube or a streaming platform, the guitar won't sound right because it is in a different overall pitch.

After you have finished adjusting the Low E, place a finger on the 5th fret of the string and tune the second string (the A) to that pitch, as shown in the diagram below:

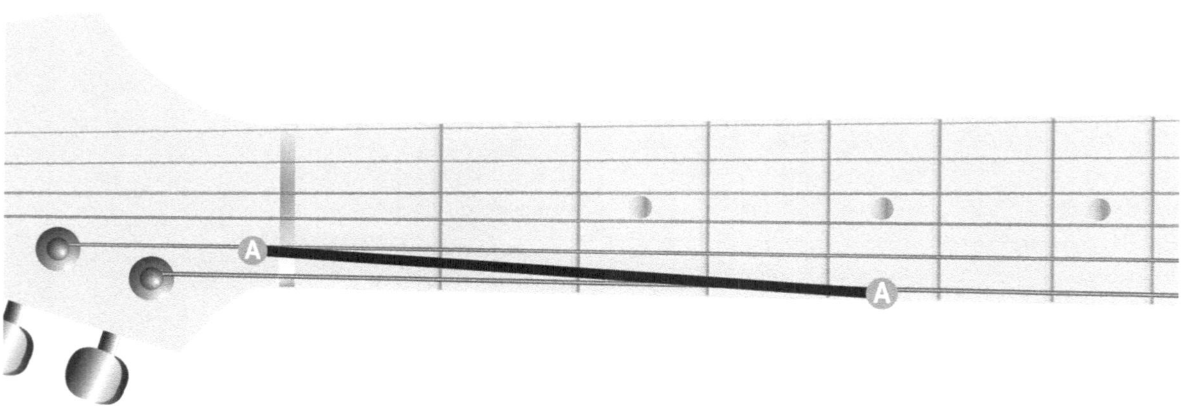

If the note is flat, turn the tuning head (usually counter-clockwise) to sharpen it until it is the same as the note on the fifth fret of the Low E string. If it is sharp, turn the tuning head to lower the tension and flatten the note until it is the same as the fifth fret of the Low E.

It's now time to move on to the next open string - the D. To tune this, place your finger on the fifth fret of the A string above it, as shown below:

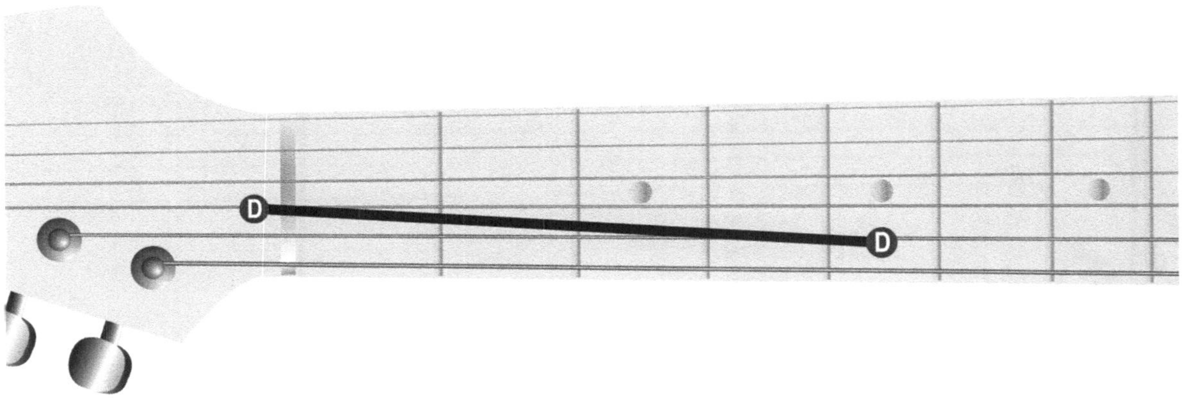

As with the first string we tuned, adjust it by making it either sharper or flatter until it is the same as the fretted note.

Now go through exactly the same process, but down one more string, to get the next string - the G - in tune.

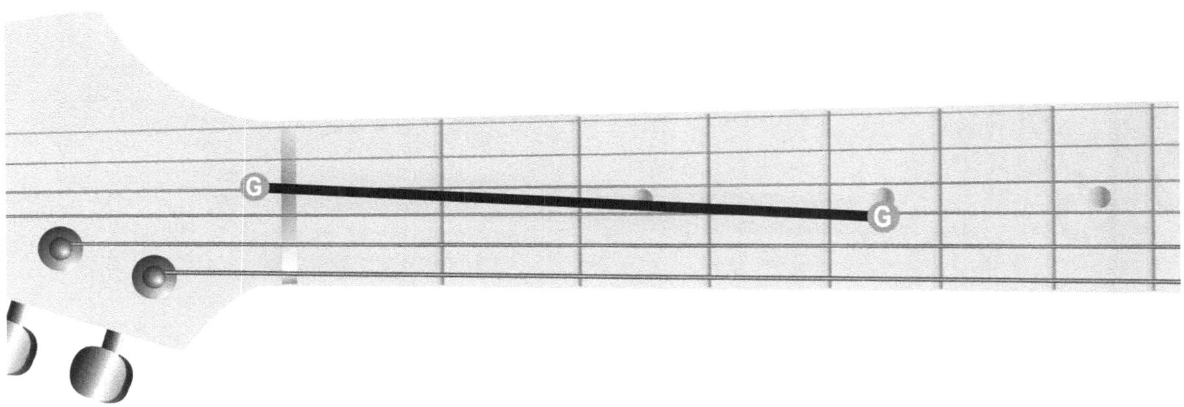

It's now time to tune the B string. This time, put your first finger on the fourth fret of the G string, not the fifth, as you have done with all other strings, and sharpen or flatten it until it matches the fretted note.

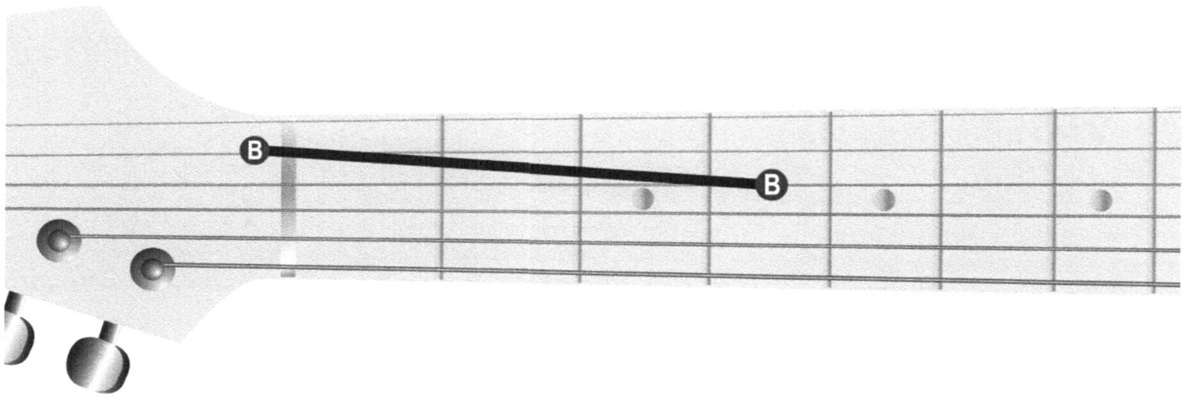

And finally, the high e string. We now go back to the fifth fret of the B string and match that note to the open string by adjusting the tuning head of the high e string.

The whole process is shown in the diagram below:

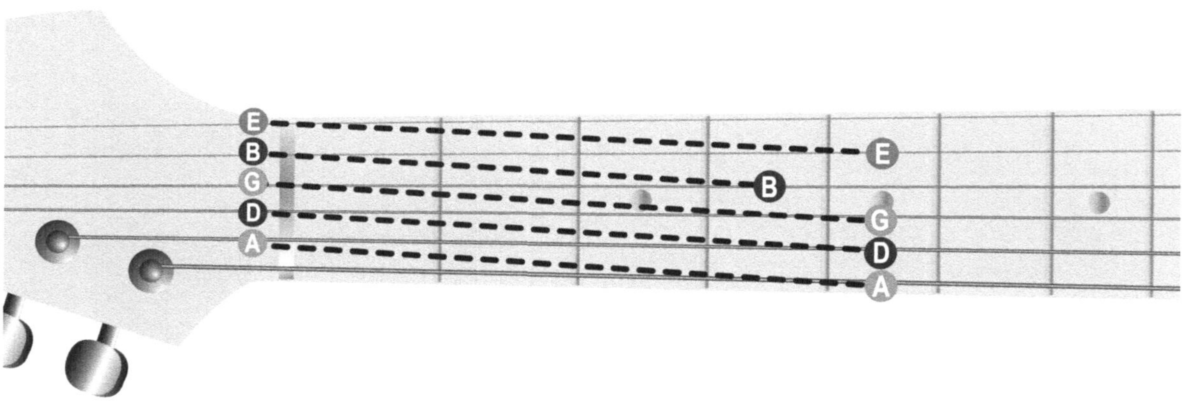

Being 100% honest, the first time anyone tries tuning by ear, they usually end up either getting totally frustrated and giving up, or the guitar sounds absolutely terrible when they have finished.

Don't worry about the outcome for now. You have gone through the process, now use your app to get the guitar perfectly in tune, and come back and have another go at tuning by ear in a few days when you're feeling less frustrated.

Tuners and apps are so quick and easy to use that I don't expect you to go through this process every time you practice, but try tuning the guitar yourself every two or three days, then check the results with your tuner.

Over time, you will notice that you are getting the strings closer and closer to perfect tuning using only your ear, which shows that your musicality is improving. In six months, you'll be tuning by ear without even thinking about it.

Acquiring this skill takes time because you have to develop your ears to accurately pick out the pitch of each note, but it's well worth the effort - who knows when your next chance of beach party stardom will be?

How often should you tune?

Guitars can go out of tune very easily; even a gentle knock or a slight change of temperature can affect the tuning. You therefore need to tune your guitar every time you play it. Plus, remember to quickly double-check the tuning after you've tuned it to make sure every string is still in tune.

Let's now move on to the next Chapter, where we'll make a lot more noise…

CHAPTER 2
LET'S PLAY A TUNE
HOW TO PLAY YOUR FIRST NOTES CLEANLY AND CONFIDENTLY

Before we get to our first melody, there are a few more basics that we need to cover, starting with…

HOW AND WHERE TO PLAY A NOTE

You've already been playing notes while learning to tune by ear, but have you been doing it correctly? Let's find out…

Yes, there is a wrong way and a right way to do something as simple as playing a note. Get this right, and everything you play, especially your chords, will sound much better.

So, what's the secret?

Well, there are two; the first is to use your fingertip, but bent slightly towards you. This is the most natural position for your hand, so if you're already doing it, congratulations.

However, some beginners try and keep their fingers straight, which is a bad technique. Simply relax and flex your first finger and use its tip to push down into the fretboard, not too hard, but hard enough to produce a nice, clear note.

As you improve, you will find that you don't need to press anywhere near as hard as you do now, so don't worry if you think you are pressing too hard; you will gradually press more gently as your skills develop.

Don't use a flattened finger to play a note at this stage; we will be doing this later as things get a little more complex, but for now, one fingertip in the right place will get you a crystal clear note. For reference, the following picture shows what your fingertip should be doing…

Pic 20 - Fingertip in the perfect position

Secondly, even though the frets seem to be quite close together, especially near the top of the fingerboard, there is, in fact, a lot more room between them than you realize. To get the best-sounding note, you need to put your finger in a precise position between the frets, not just anywhere.

For example, try playing the first fret of the low E string with your finger pushing up against the nut (the thin piece of plastic or bone that separates the neck from the headstock and holds the strings in place).

It's difficult to press the string down in this position, and the note probably sounds muffled unless you use a lot of force.

Now move the finger to just before the first fret wire on the same string. It is still the same note on the same fret, but now it is much easier to press down, and more than likely sounds a lot better.

You need to get your finger as close to the fret wire that is furthest from the nut of each fret whenever you are playing, and this is especially important for playing chords. The closer you are, the better the note will sound.

However, you can't go too far - if you play on top of or over a fret, you will once again get a muffled sound.

Here are a few pictures showing you what not to do…

Pic 21 - Wrong finger position, too far from the fret

Pic 22 - Wrong finger position, on top of a fret

We took a brief look at TAB in the last chapter, but let's now explore it a bit more as we begin…

READING TAB

You already know that the six lines in a TAB diagram represent the six strings and that a zero placed on one of them means that you need to play that string open. But TAB can be used to show us a lot more than that, as we are about to find out.

Tablature, or TAB for short, is a simple way of writing and reading musical information for the guitar or other fretted instruments.

As opposed to learning to read music in the traditional way, which can take weeks (or even months), TAB is far easier to understand because what you see on the page is what you see on the guitar.

Here is a simple example, again, don't worry about the musical stave at the top, that's just for reference and to show how much easier TAB is to read…

Exercise 2

As we've already seen, there are six lines in TAB as opposed to the five in a musical stave. And, as you also know, each line corresponds to a string on the guitar, with the line closest to you in the TAB being the string closest to you when you look down on the instrument, i.e., the low E string, and the furthest line away being the high e string.

But what do all the numbers mean?

The numbers on the lines correspond with the frets you need to play.

The first note is number '0' on the fourth line from the bottom of the diagram, which is a note you've already played in the first exercise, so play that open note again on the G string - the fourth string as you look down on the guitar.

The second note is number '1' on the fifth string from the bottom of the TAB diagram; therefore, you play the first fret on the B string (the fifth string as you look down on the guitar neck).

Next, we have a '0' on the same line. Again, you are familiar with this and need to play the open B string before playing the first fret on the same string (the B) once more, indicated by the number '1'.

We now move to another line, the sixth one from the bottom of the diagram, which represents the high e string, the thinnest of them all. Again, the number '0' indicates that you should play the open high e string, before returning to the B string to play number '3' - the third fret.

Now, go back to the beginning of the TAB and play all those notes once again, but this time carry on playing the other notes as indicated in the TAB until you get to the end.

Do you recognize the notes?

I'm sure you know this melody; you hear it during every New Year celebration. Yes, it's the beginning of Auld Lang Syne.

Not only have you learned quite a bit more about reading guitar tablature, but you have also just played your first melody. Now play it a few more times so that it gets easier, and perfect the phrasing so that it sounds exactly like Auld Lang Syne.

Note: There's a lot more to TAB than I've covered here. Not only can it be used to show notes, but you can also show which chords to play, including symbols to represent slides, hammer-ons, pull-offs, or any other technique.
If next to nothing in the last sentence made sense, don't worry, it will all be covered as we move through the series, but for now, you know the basics of TAB.

BACK TO THE MELODY

Let's now take another look at the melody, now that you're a little bit more familiar with it.

I know that you've already played this a few times, but have you been playing it correctly and using the right fingers?

Using the correct finger for each note makes any melody, scale, or guitar riff far easier to play. The basic rule is…

One finger per fret within one position

The melody starts with the open note, so you don't need to have your hand on or even near the fretboard to play that. However, as with many things in life, a little bit of preparation makes the execution a lot easier. So, think of what is coming next before or as you play every note.

Start by playing the open note on the G string, but keep your first finger hovering over the first fret of the B string (the fifth from the top), ready to play it next.

You could even put it in place at the start, before you even play the first open note, but that can get a bit complex, or you might muffle the first note by touching it with the tip of your finger. Therefore, at this stage, let it hover above the note, ready to be played when the time comes.

And since you have already played the first note, that time is now, so put your finger down into position on the first fret of the B string and play the note.

Now lift the finger once more, but keep it positioned close to the string, and play the third note of the melody, the open B string. Now, place the finger back on the first fret and play that note once more.

You're glad you kept it nice and close now, aren't you?

Next, lift it again and play the next note, the open high e string.

Which brings us nicely to our first Music Theory Snippet, where I break everything down into bite-sized pieces so that it never becomes overwhelming. So, just in case you don't already know, let's take a look at Music Theory Snippet #1…

What is a Bar?

You're all thinking that a bar is a place you go for an enjoyable drink with your friends. Or maybe it's somewhere where you enjoy watching some great live music. However, in music theory, a bar doesn't involve any alcohol, but it might feature some very loud music!

A bar is a segment of music that is defined by the vertical lines on each side of it, which are called bar lines. These divide a musical staff or TAB into sections that contain a specific number of beats.

Back to the melody… here is the TAB once again, so that you don't need to constantly turn the page…

The third bar - you know what the word means now, excellent! - starts by playing the third fret on the B string. This needs to be played with the third finger.

If you recall the golden rule - **one finger per fret within one position** - since the first finger is being used to play notes on the first fret, you need to use your third finger to play notes on the third fret.

You could try and play it all with one finger, as many beginners do when first attempting a melody, but that is clumsy and inefficient, so always stick with the one finger per fret rule.

After you have played the third note on the B string, play the first fret on the same string using your first finger, before returning to the third fret for the next note. As you can see, using the first and third fingers together makes everything far easier to play.

Now move to the open high e string and play it open, before returning to the second string, the B, to use your third finger to play the note on the third fret.

Time for the fourth bar…

Start by playing the note on the first fret of the second string (B). Then repeat that note once more before moving to the high e string, where you need to play an open note, followed by one on the third fret using your third finger…

…and finally, the note on the fifth fret, which you can play with your little finger. This note is slightly outside the one fret per finger rule, but it's the most practical way of playing it.

I know that was a ridiculously complicated way of explaining how to play this melody. However, it was well worth it because you now realize everything you need to keep in mind as you play the notes of any melody or guitar riff.

Don't worry, we won't need to go into anywhere near that much detail for future melodies.

Let's finish this chapter by adding a few more bars to the TAB and playing the melody all the way through, as shown below…

Exercise 3

Start from the beginning, using all the tips and tricks I just shared to play it in the most efficient way. Then continue until the end using the same techniques.

To download the audio files for the exercises mentioned in this section, head to **playfirstnote.com/bonuses.**

CHAPTER 3

LET'S GET THOSE FINGERS MOVING

MORE MELODIES AND EXERCISES

Hopefully, you're enjoying playing Auld Lang Syne and can't wait till next New Year's Eve to show off your new guitar skills. But we need something to impress everyone before then, so let's take a look at some more melodies to get those fingers working.

MELODY 1 - LONDON BRIDGE

This is a bit more complex than Auld Lang Syne, but with a little practice, you should get your fingers around it.

However, it's easy to know which fingers to use: use the first finger for every note on the 1st fret, the second for the notes on the 2nd fret, and the third finger for the notes on the 3rd fret.

For the final two bars, play the note on the 1st fret with your first finger, then the note on the 2nd fret of the B string with your third finger, the note on the 2nd fret of the G string with your second finger, and the note on the second fret of the D string with your first finger to form an A chord (we'll be covering that in the next chapter) to finish the melody.

MELODY 2 - FOR HE'S A JOLLY GOOD FELLOW

Here's a longer melody for you to wrap your fingers around, but quite a few of the bars are repeated, making it easier to play and remember.

There is also a new bit of TAB included. You'll notice in Bar 9 that there are two '0's on the G string with a curved line connecting them. You need to play the open string and then let the note ring; therefore, the second '0' doesn't need to be played.

Unless indicated differently, it's the same for all notes connected with a curved line.

To download the audio files for the melodies and exercises mentioned in this section, head to **playfirstnote.com/bonuses.**

MELODY 3 - HOUSE OF THE RISING SUN

For our final melody, we have the classic House of the Rising Sun. We're raising the bar a little with this one, because you'll need to change your hand position a few times to get to the higher notes.

It's a bit tougher, isn't it? This is because you need to change hand position to go up to the 5th fret of the high e string for the second note, and a few more times later on.

However, since the first note is an open E, start with your hand hovering above the 5th fret, ready to play the second note with your third finger, before returning to the open B string. This will give you a bit of time to get your hand back in position for the notes in the third and fourth bars.

It's now back up to the 5th fret, and again, play the note with your third finger, then use your first finger for the notes on the 3rd fret of the high e string, before taking your hand off once more for the open notes.

Bars 8 and 9 also contain notes on the 5th, as well as the 4th fret, but once again, there are open strings before and after them, so there shouldn't be any serious problems. From then on, every note is within the first four frets, which makes playing it a little easier.

EXERCISES

Getting your fingers moving efficiently is one of the most important aspects of learning the guitar. Repetition and practice is the key, but you need to make sure that what you are practising is getting you results in as short a time as possible.

This is why exercises are so important… Oh no! Exercises!!!

Finger exercises, much like the exercises most people despise doing at their local gym, have a very bad reputation. Most people think that they are boring, and to be perfectly honest, they're right; they are a little boring. But the results they produce speak for themselves, so they are well worth incorporating into your daily practice routine.

The best way to get over the 'This is boring' mindset while doing exercises is to think of them as a warm-up routine - something you go through to get your hands ready for the 'real' work.

Plus, limit how long you practice them. For beginners, you should only be doing one exercise per day, for a maximum of three minutes.

In my opinion, it's well worth spending 180 seconds of your day to get your hands and fingers working like you've been playing for years in a matter of months. The rewards really do outweigh the effort, so stick with it; you'll be amazed at how quickly you'll see results.

Let's start with one of the most fun…

THE SIMPLE SPIDER EXERCISE

This exercise gets more complex as your skills improve, but to get you started, we'll go with the simplest version, as shown in the TAB below:

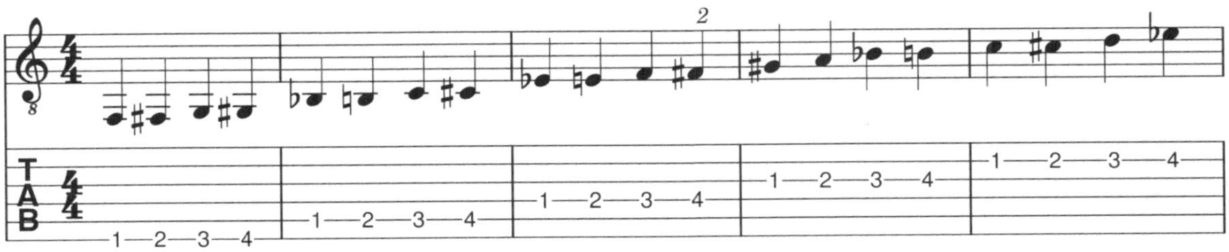

This, and the more complex versions created from it, is one of the best warm-up exercises around. It is widely used by guitar legends in their live and recording warm-ups; it really is that effective.

It's great for cementing the one finger per fret rule and for increasing your finger independence, making everything you play on the instrument easier and, eventually, almost effortless.

Start by playing the note on the 1st fret of the low E string with your first finger, then play the note on the 2nd fret with your second finger, the 3rd with your third finger, and the 4th fret with your little finger.

Now repeat the same sequence on the A string, the D string, the G string, the B string, and the high e string. Before going back down the strings until you return to your starting position, back on the low E string. Here's the TAB again for reference:

Now move your whole hand up one fret, and play the note on the 2nd fret of the Low E string with your first finger, the note on the 3rd fret with your second finger, the 4th fret with your third finger, and finally, the note on the 5th fret with your little finger.

Now go down a string and repeat the note sequence using the same fingers on the A string, followed by the D string, the G string, the B string, and then the high e string. Then come back down the strings playing the same sequence until you once again return to the Low E string.

The two sections of the exercise that we've covered so far are shown in the following TAB:

To download the audio files for the exercises mentioned in this section, head to **playfirstnote.com/bonuses.**

Now, move your whole hand up another fret and play the 3rd fret on the Low E string using your first finger, then the 4th using your second finger, the 5th using your third finger, and the 6th fret using your little finger.

Then repeat on the A, D, G, B, and high E strings before returning down the strings to the Low E string once again, as shown in the following TAB:

Continue up one fret at a time until you have played the exercise for three minutes.

Do the exercise slowly, concentrating on absolute perfection; this isn't about speed, that will come as you play things perfectly.

Concentrate on making every note sound crystal clear and holding it until you are ready to play the next one; this will make your fingers as strong as Arnie in his prime.

Three minutes per day as a start to your practice routine is all that's needed to see results in as little as a few weeks, so concentrate on doing it to the very best of your abilities.

Alternate Picking

There are a few ways to pick a note. I'm not talking about where you should play a note or how to hold your pick; we've already covered that. It's now time to discuss the direction your pick is going in.

Most beginners start by picking every note downwards. However, this is very inefficient because you strike a string with your pick, which then makes contact with the string, and then ends up below it.

You now lift the pick back up over the string, before repeating the motion to play the next note - as I said, very inefficient.

Alternate picking is a far more sensible way of playing notes. Start by picking the first note you need to play with a downstroke. Now, instead of moving your finger back up over the string, strike the string with an upward motion to play the second note.

Now move to the next note and strike it downwards, and then the next, which you strike with an upstroke.

This down-up-down-up pick motion is twice as efficient as playing every note with a downstroke. Therefore, always use it when playing and especially when practising exercises.

There are exceptions to alternate picking, which we will be covering later on in this series, but for now, always alternate pick everything you play for the most efficient and fluid motion.

Metronome - Your Perfect Rhythm Buddy

To get the best results from this and every other exercise, you should be playing along with a metronome, but it's still very early days, so it isn't 100% necessary yet.

But for those who want to start as they mean to go on, here's what you need to know...

Metronomes have changed a lot from the classic pyramidal designs with a big swinging arm, which you often see on top of pianos. You can either get an electronic one, which is similar in size to a guitar tuner, or, better still, and for free, download a metronome app onto your smartphone.

Metronomes are your rhythm buddy as you practice, your drummer in a box. But they are a lot less crazy than most drummers I have played with! They will massively improve your rhythm and sense of musical time, cementing everything you play into a steady rhythm.

How to Use a Metronome

Once you've downloaded an app, open it and set the speed to 60 beats per minute, i.e., one beat per second. This is the golden number to begin all exercises, regardless of what level your guitar playing is at.

Listen to the beat and get into its rhythm; you're about to start playing along with it. But don't play a note on every beat, play on every other beat.

Familiarize yourself with the beat, then play the first note - the first fret of the Low E string - on the next beat and hold it as you listen to the following beat, then play the next note - the second fret of the Low E string - on the next beat, hold it again as you listen to the following beat, before playing the next note - the third fret of the Low E string.

Continue doing this for the full three minutes of the exercise.

Note: The reason you are playing on every other beat, and not every beat, is that the beat you are listening to but not playing on keeps you in perfect time. If you play on every beat, you could be playing slightly ahead of time, or slightly behind it, and you have nothing to reference; therefore, you would just be solidifying your sloppy sense of rhythm.

Pedal to the Metal

After you've played the exercise for a few days and it's a lot easier, you can increase the speed of the metronome - try 63 beats per minute. The difference is so small that you won't notice, but it is ever so slightly faster.

If, after a few more days, you can play the exercise perfectly - no missed notes, no fumbles, every note crystal clear and held until its time to play the next note, and using strict alternate picking, then you can increase the speed of the metronome once again - try 67 beats per minute.

Then play it at this speed for a few days until it is perfect, before again increasing the speed - let's say to 70 beats per minute. However, if you can't play the exercise absolutely perfectly, then you need to go back a step and master it at the slower speed before raising the speed once more.

Over time, you will be playing this, and any other exercise, scale, or whatever you are learning, at breakneck speed. And because you have spent the time to play it perfectly with the metronome at all speeds, not only will it be blindingly fast, but it will also be absolutely perfect.

Next, we have the…

FINGER STRENGTH EXERCISE - PRESS-UPS FOR YOUR FINGERS

There are a few different versions of this exercise, which target different pairs of fingers. We'll begin with one using the first and second fingers.

Start by placing your first finger on the 5th fret of the D string, then place your second finger on the 6th fret of the same string. Now place your third finger on the 7th fret of the G string, and your little finger on the 8th fret of the G string.

This is your starting position and is shown in the diagram below:

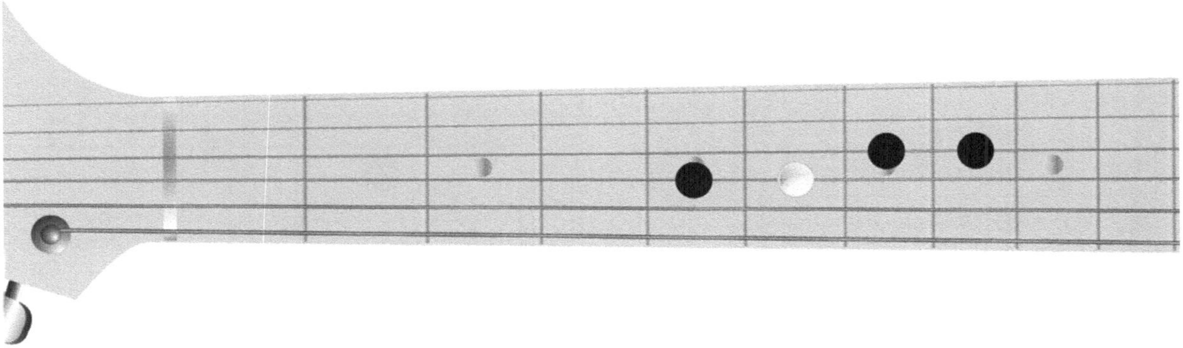

Note: Most exercises are played on or around the 5th fret because this is the most comfortable position for your arm, wrist, and hand.

Start by playing the D string using a downstroke; your fingers are already in position, so there is nothing to worry about there since you are already playing the note. Now, lift your second finger and play the D string again with an upstroke.

Then put your second finger back down and play the string again, lift and play again, put it back down, and play again, etc., remembering to use strict alternate picking throughout.

Yay! Your second finger is doing press-ups.

This exercise not only builds strength in your fingers but also aids finger independence, so that your fingers can work independently of each other, a crucial skill for guitarists.

Practice it for three minutes at the beginning of your practice sessions, alternating daily with the Spider Exercise.

It's best to do it with a metronome, but not absolutely necessary - start at 60 beats per minute and increase the speed slowly every few days. And, remember that you need to do strict alternate picking - down-up-down-up.

More Press-ups for Your Fingers

There are five finger pairs that you can use to do press-ups, the first and second, which we've just covered, the...

Second and Third - move your first finger down a string and your third finger up to get the starting position, then lift and lower your third finger, as shown below:

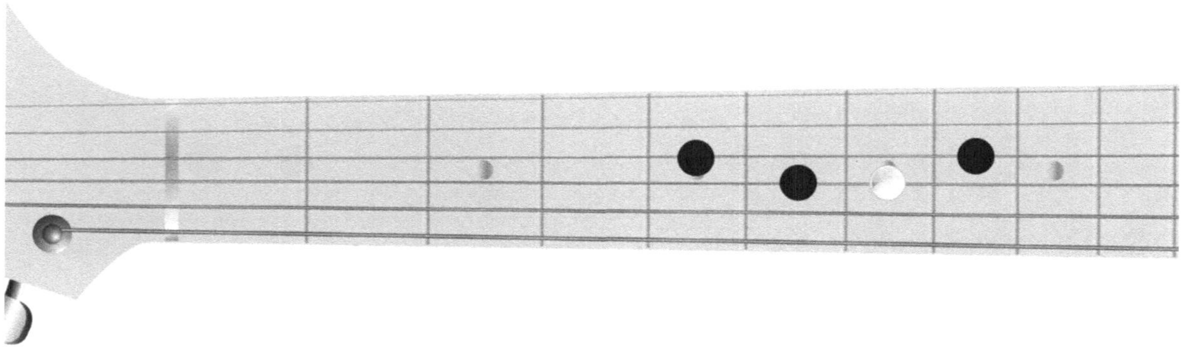

Third and Fourth - move your second finger down a string and your little finger up one to get the starting position, then lift and lower your little finger.

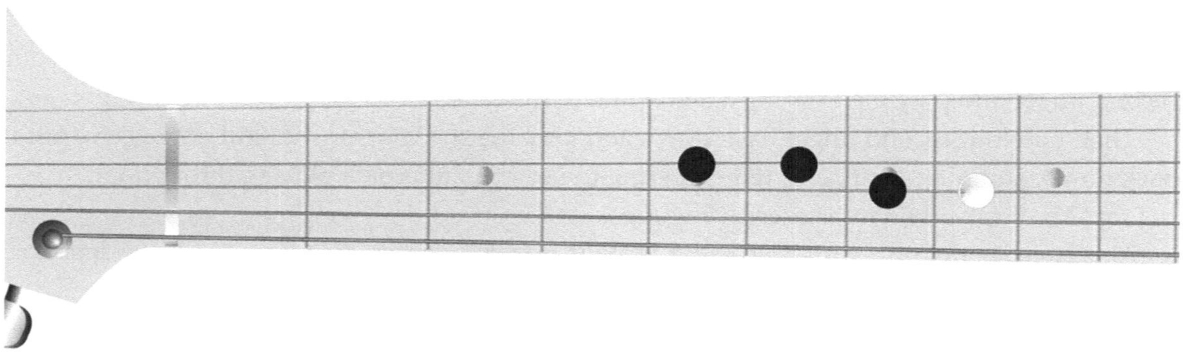

First and Third - move your first finger up a string and your little finger down one to get the starting position, then lift and lower your third finger.

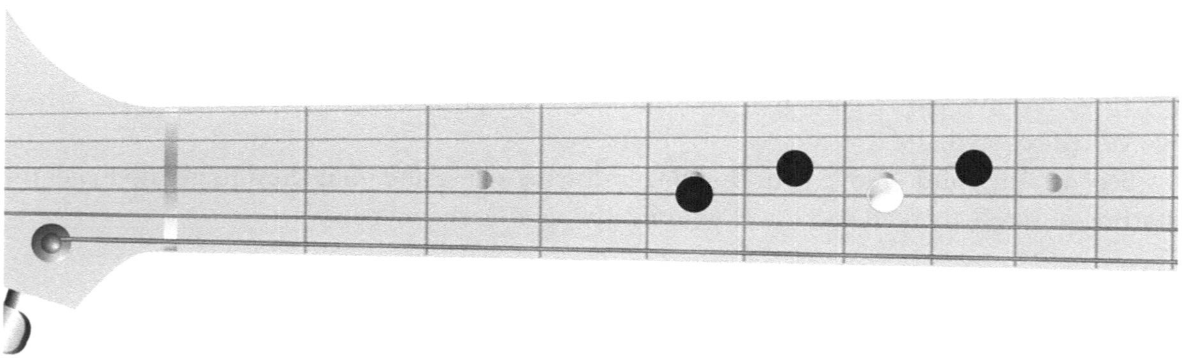

Second and Fourth - move your first finger down a string, your second finger up a string, your third finger down a string, and your little finger up one to get the starting position, then lift and lower your little finger.

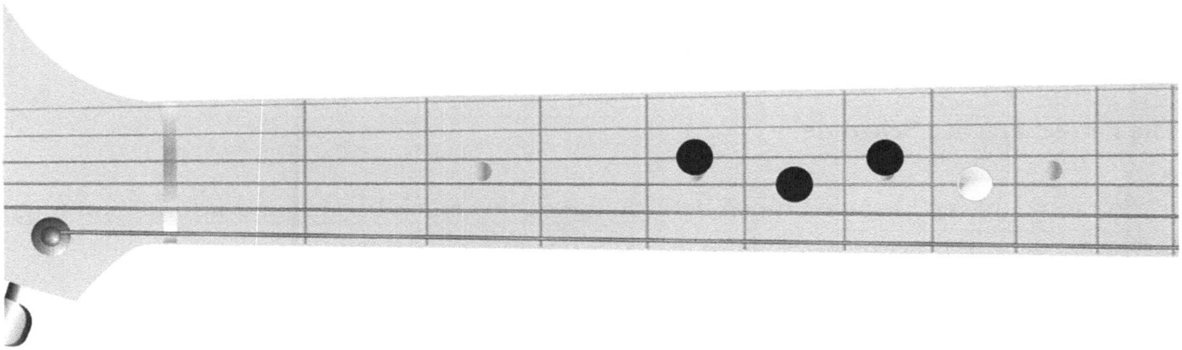

To download the audio files for the exercises mentioned in this section, head to **playfirstnote.com/bonuses.**

MORE EXERCISES

More complex versions of the Spider exercise, as well as more finger strength, dexterity, independence, and stretching exercises, will be featured in Book 2 of this series and future volumes.

Let's now move on to…

THE ART OF PRACTICE

This will be discussed in much more detail in later books, but for now, here are the most important things to remember.

20 Minutes is All You Need

This constantly surprises anyone who is learning the guitar, but the fact is that if you do 20 minutes of extremely focused practice five days a week, every week, your improvement is guaranteed.

That's right, you only need to spend 20 minutes a day to become a great guitarist!

However, you'll notice that I used the words 'extremely focused'; this is the key. Noodling for 20 minutes, playing a little bit of this and a little bit of some other song that you know isn't practising.

You have to play things that you can't already play, and you have to play them with conviction and the goal of perfection. That means that as soon as you can play anything well - a scale, a song, a particular technique, whatever - you can no longer include it in your practice sessions.

The Perfect Practice Schedule

So far, we haven't covered much because there is so much background information to go through, but your practice schedule could look something like this:

	M.M. Speed	Time	M	T	W	T	F
Spider Exercise	60	3 mins					
Finger Strength - 1 & 2	60	3 mins					
Auld Lang Syne Melody	N/A	2 mins					
London Bridge Melody	N/A	3 mins					
For He's a Jolly Good Fellow Melody	N/A	3 mins					
House of the Rising Sun Melody	N/A	3 mins					

To download a blank printable PDF of the weekly practice schedule, please go to **playfirstnote.com/bonuses.**

Instead of the recommended 20 minutes, we'll start with a 17-minute practice schedule, but we'll be adding lots more to it soon. Even so, you'll notice that there is a lot that you can get done in 17 minutes of focused practice.

In reality, this practice schedule will be a little longer than 17 minutes because you'll need to take a short break between each task to prepare for the next one. However, with time, this shouldn't be more than 15 to 30 seconds, which will only add a few extra minutes to the total length.

Practice Notes

- To get the schedule up to 17 minutes, I've included two different finger exercises, which may be too much for some beginners at this early stage. If you find that you're not enjoying doing two exercises per day, do one and vary it daily. You should also vary the finger pairs of the Finger Strength Press Up exercise every time.
- I've included Monday to Friday as the practice days, giving you the weekend off. But you can do whatever suits you best, take a Wednesday off for a mid-week break, or do more on the weekend when you have some free time and take two weeknights off.
- Don't beat yourself up if you miss a day, especially in the early days, until practising becomes part of your schedule. You can catch up by doing two sessions at different times on another day. But don't take all five weekdays off and then cram five different sessions in over the weekend. You will learn at a far better rate by doing a series of short 20-minute sessions on different days than by doing an hour and 40 minutes on a Saturday.

Let's now move on to the next chapter, which has a lot more goodies to fill up your practice schedule...

CHAPTER 4

LET'S LEARN SOME CHORDS!

YOUR FIRST FIVE CHORDS AND HOW TO PLAY THEM CLEANLY

Chords are the building blocks of every song you know and love. So it's time to take a look at five of the most important ones you'll ever learn - A, C, D, E, and G.

But as usual, there are a few things to go over before we get to that, starting with…

READING CHORDS USING TAB

You already know how melodies are written using TAB and how to read them, so let's learn how to recognize and read chords.

You can spot chords in tablature because you will see a series of numbers stacked directly on top of each other on the different TAB lines, as shown below…

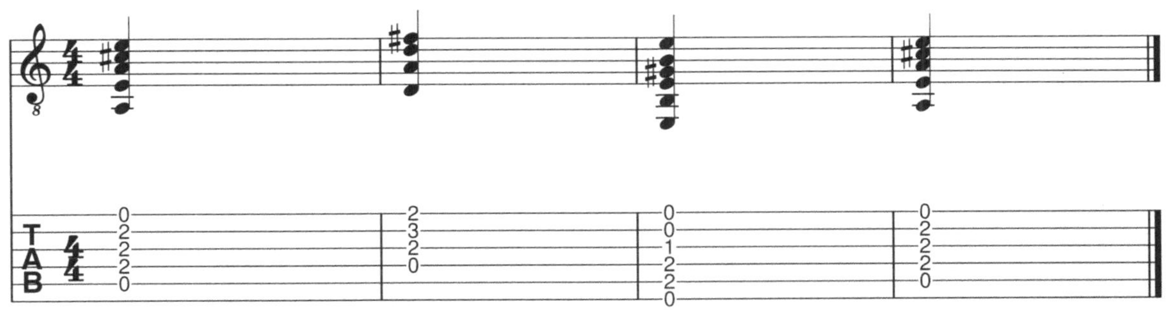

Since the notes are all in a line, you play them all together, i.e., you play a chord that contains all the notes shown on the TAB.

Have a go at playing them, they probably won't sound great yet, but I'll be showing you not only how to play them properly but also how to quickly change between them after Music Theory Snippet #2…

What is a Chord?

A chord is a combination of three or more notes that are played at the same time to create a combined sound.

They are used in songs and other pieces of music to form the tonal foundation over which melodies, harmonies, riffs, solos, etc. are played.

As well as in TAB, chords can also be shown in Chord Boxes, as shown below:

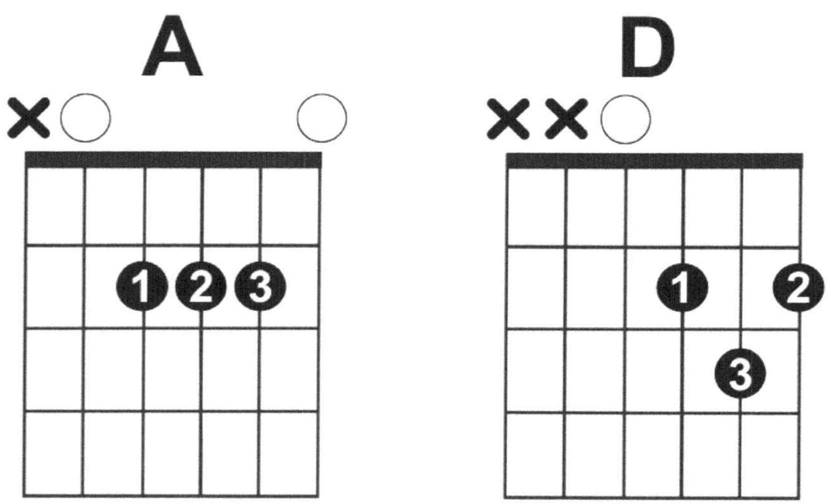

A chord box represents the top four frets of the neck of the guitar, with the thick black line being the nut. The six vertical lines represent the six strings going from left to right - Low E - A - D - G - B - High E.

If you see an '**X**' above a vertical line, then you don't need to play that string, while an '**O**' means that you need to play the open string. The black circles indicate where you should place your fingers, with which finger to use shown by the number within the circle.

Now that you know what they look like, let's…

LEARN HOW TO PLAY CHORDS

We'll start at the beginning of the alphabet with an A chord, which is shown below:

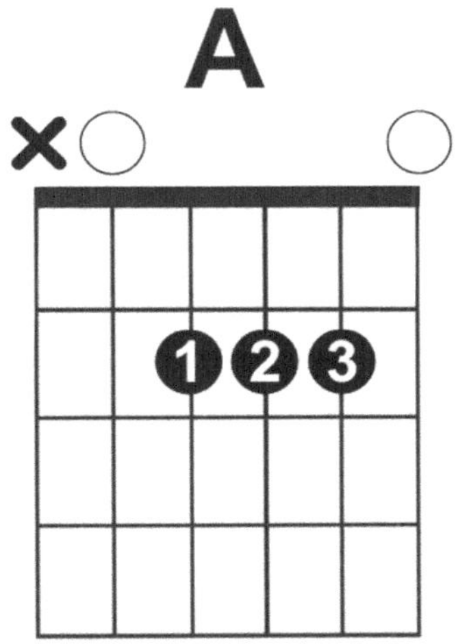

Start by putting your first finger on the 2nd fret of the fourth (D) string, then put your second finger on the 2nd fret of the third (G) string, and now put your third finger on the 2nd fret of the second (B) string, as shown below...

Pic 23 - A Chord

It's quite a squeeze, isn't it?

Give it a strum, it probably doesn't sound great.

Now, try playing every string one at a time to see how they sound. Start with the A string (you don't need to play the Low E, there is an '**X**' next to it), then the D, the G, the B, and the high E string to finish.

It usually sounds terrible, with nearly every note being muffled, but don't worry about that. Now take your fingers off the chord and relax.

You've just played your first chord - an A Major - congratulations!

It didn't sound great, but it will in a few days.

Let's play it again, so put your fingers back in the same position. Give it another strum, then pick all the strings once again. Now relax once more. Repeat this four or five more times until you're comfortable playing the chord.

The D Chord

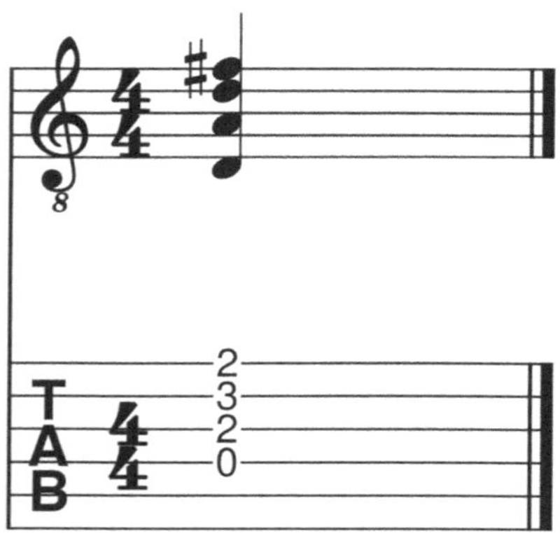

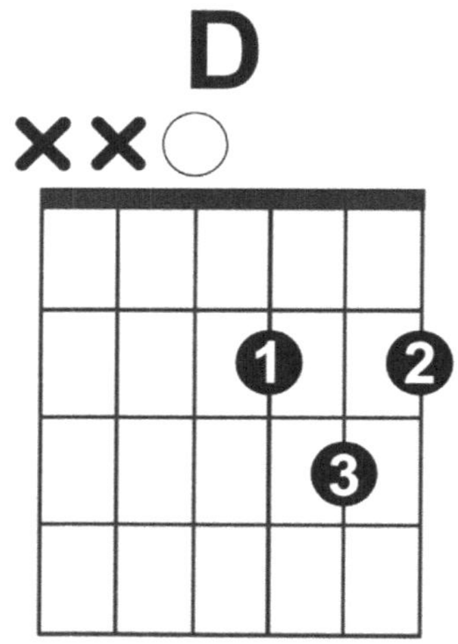

Most beginners find the D major chord easier to play than the A because you are not squashing all your fingers into such a small space.

Start by placing your first finger onto the 2nd fret of the G string, your second finger onto the 2nd fret of the high e string, and then your third finger onto the 3rd fret of the B string. Your fingers should have created a triangular shape as shown in the chord box and in the picture below…

Pic 24 - D Chord

Give it a strum, then pick each string as we did for the A chord, remembering to only pick the four thinnest strings; the two thickest ones have an '**X**' next to them, so don't need to be played.

It should sound slightly better than the A chord you just played, with less muffled notes.

Take another break, then put your fingers back in the same positions and strum and pick it four or five more times.

It's now time to learn…

The E Chord

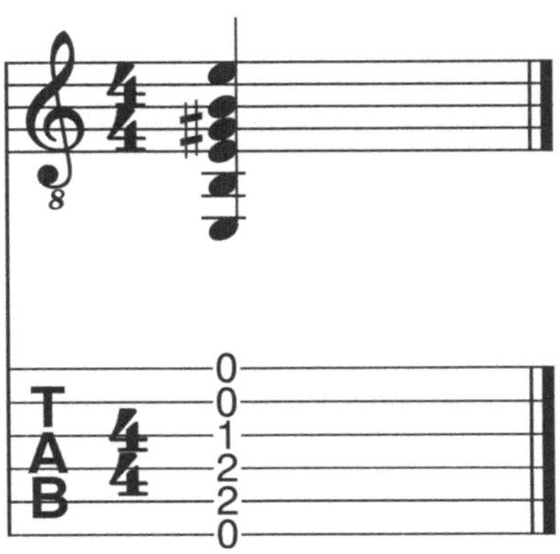

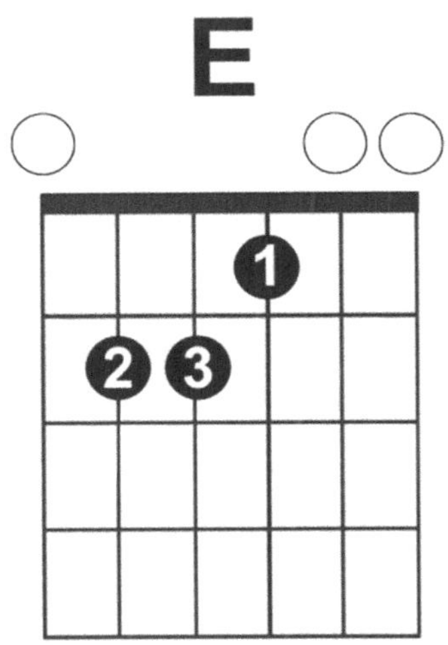

This is again a little easier than the A chord. To play an E major chord, start by placing your first finger on the 1st fret of the G string, then add your second finger to the 2nd fret of the A string and your third finger to the 2nd fret of the D string, as shown below…

Pic 25 - E Chord

Once again, give it a strum, then play each string one at a time - Low E - A - D - G - B - High e. Repeat this with rests four or five times.

Repetition is the Key

Now go back to the first chord A, and strum and pick every string a few more times, followed by a D chord, then back again to the E. Repeat until you memorize the chord shapes and they start sounding better.

As a break from all this chord playing, here's Music Theory Snippet #3…

What is a Major Chord?

A Major chord is a combination of three different notes that are played at the same time to create a combined sound. On a guitar, they can consist of three, four, five, or six notes, but the additional notes are repeats of the three notes that make up the chord.

They consist of the first, third, and fifth notes of the

major scale, but you don't need to worry about that for now. They have a joyful, happy sound and are the mainstay of most popular songs.

Major chords are normally simply referred to by their note name, i.e., A major is usually called an A, D major is also known as D, etc.

Time for a Massive Sonic Improvement

Now that you've memorized our first three chords and become more familiar with playing them, let's spend some time getting the chords to sound better.

This might happen quickly or could take you a few days, or even a week. So be patient and spend your time trying to make every string within each chord sound crystal clear.

First, the A major chord...

Unlike the first time you played it, let's approach it differently and start with the B string, the second thinnest, so put your third finger down on the 2nd fret.

Don't worry about the other two fingers for now; we'll add them soon. Put your finger right next to the fretwire that is furthest from the nut and press straight down with your fingertip turned slightly towards you, as your hand naturally lies, as shown below:

Pic 26 - The third finger playing an A chord.

Now play the note; it should ring out clearly. If it doesn't, you either need to move it slightly, press a little harder, or both. Adjust it until it produces a nice, crystal clear note when you pick it.

Congrats, one down, four to go (A major is played using only five notes)...

Keeping your third finger in position, now try playing the open high e string. It might ring out straight away; if so, well done. If not, and it sounds muffled, you more than likely need to move your third finger slightly so that it isn't touching the high e string and muting it as shown in the two pictures below.

Pics 27 - Correct - the third finger is not touching the high e string

Pic 28 - Incorrect - the third finger is touching the high e string.

In the first, the high e string is left to ring; in the second, it is muted by the underside of the tip of the third finger.

If your third finger isn't touching the e string, but the note is still muffled, you need to check to see if another part of your hand is touching it, causing it to be muted. This is shown in the picture below of the full A chord, where the point where the first finger meets the palm is holding the neck, causing the high e string to be muted.

Pic 29 - Muting the high e string with the fleshy part of the first finger.

If this is the case, move your hand away from the high e string until it sounds clear.

Now return to the B string to make sure that it is still nice and clear. If so, play it and then the high e string, and you should now have two clear notes.

Two down, three to go!

Keeping your third finger in position, it's time to move on to the second finger, so add it to the 2nd fret of the G string.

Again, you need to position it as close to the fretwire as possible; therefore, it needs to be pressed tight against your third finger. Play the note. If it sounds great, congrats. If not, move the finger slightly or press a little harder until the note rings out clearly, as shown below...

Pic 30 - Second and third fingers of an A chord in the perfect position

Now, check the notes on the B and E strings once more to make sure that they are still clear. If so, play all three notes in turn. If not, make adjustments to your fingers until all the notes sound great.

Three down, two to go!

It's now time to add your first finger to the 2nd fret of the D string.

As always, you need to get it as close to the fretwire as possible, but that's quite difficult because you have two other fingers in the way. Therefore, push it hard against your second finger; you might also need to press down a little bit harder to get a clear note.

Pic 31 - The first, second, and third fingers of an A chord in the perfect position

When you get a crystal clear note on the D string, check the other three strings to make sure that they still sound good.

Nearly there…

All your fingers are in place, but you need to check the open A string to make sure that it's clear and true.

There is no finger on it, so it shouldn't be a problem, but you could be touching it with the tip of your first finger, causing it to sound muffled. If so, move your first finger down slightly.

Once the A string is sounding great, check all the other notes and make any adjustments as needed to get a perfect chord. Give it a strum, sounds great, doesn't it?

I know that was a lot of work, but it will pay dividends in the future. The better your chords sound, the more you will want to play and practice. And the more you play, the better you will become, making you want to play and practice even more.

You need to go through this process with every chord you learn, but there is no rush; spend a few minutes perfecting one chord one day, then move on to another on the next.

Over time, you will develop Muscle Memory, and your fingers will instinctively know where they should be for every chord you play.

THE 1-2-3-4 CHORD CHANGE EXERCISE

Now that you know the chords that we'll be using for our first chord progressions, rhythm patterns, and songs, let's see how fast you can change between them.

If you're using a metronome, set it to 60; if not, simply count 1-2-3-4 out loud, with every number being about a second apart.

Count to 4, then on the following '1', play an A chord, then change it to a D chord and strum downwards on the next '1' - if possible - then change to E, and strum down on '1' - if possible - then back to A.

Do this for a few minutes to see how quickly you can change between the chords.

But once again, don't worry, this might take a few hours or a few days to start sounding good. But every time you play it, there will be a slight improvement; you might not notice it, but you will be getting fractionally faster every time.

As the chord changes get easier, increase the metronome speed or count a little more quickly.

To download the audio files for the exercises mentioned in this section, head to **playfirstnote.com/bonuses.**

There's More than One Way to... Conquer Chords

When learning any new chords, it's important to practice them in two distinct ways. The first is slowly and carefully, aiming for perfection. Strumming, then playing each note, one after the other, making sure every one of them is crystal clear.

But you also need to throw caution to the wind and take quick, blind stabs at the chords. This is why the 1-2-3-4 exercise we just went through is so valuable.

Over time, both methods become one, and not only will you be changing chords lightning fast, but also playing them perfectly.

MASTERING THE CHORD CHANGE - TIPS AND TRICKS

There are two things that you need to bear in mind when changing chords: shared fingers and anchor notes on the same string. I will be covering shared fingers in Book 2 of this series as your chord vocabulary grows, so let's concentrate on...

Anchor Notes on the Same String

Let's say that we want to quickly change from A to D. At the moment, you are taking every finger off the fretboard and then placing each one back in its new position. This is fine for some chords because it's the only way that you can change between them.

However, it's possible to make the A to D chord change far more efficient.

Start by playing the chord as normal, but now, instead of lifting all three fingers, only lift your first and second fingers, leaving your third finger in place.

Now slide the third finger up one fret from the 2nd to the 3rd, and put your first and second fingers back on the fretboard in the correct positions to make the D chord.

It's a bit complicated the first few times you try it, but with a little practice, it makes the chord change so much quicker and easier.

Try it five or six times until you get the hang of it.

And it works in reverse as well!

That's right, to go from a D to an A, play the D chord, lift your first and second fingers, move the third finger back one fret, and put the first and second fingers back in position to form an A chord. Now practice going from A to D, back to A, for a few minutes until it becomes easy.

Changing from an E to a D

The same technique can be used to change from an E chord to a D chord.

Start by playing an E chord, then instead of lifting all three fingers, only lift the second and third. Now slide the first finger up one fret and then place the second and third fingers in position to create a D chord. Reverse the process to go back to an E chord.

Unfortunately, there are no cheats to make the chord change from an A to an E any easier, so you'll just have to lift all three fingers and then put them all back down again. Sorry about that.

QUICK CHANGE CHORD EXERCISE

This is a fantastic exercise to get your chord changes up to the speed needed to play songs, so do your very best to play this as fast as possible.

This is primarily a speed-based exercise, but do try and make the chords sound good; they'll need to when you are playing songs.

It's simple enough to play and remember. Start by playing an E chord, then adjusting your fingers, slide up one fret to create the D chord, and strum that. Now, re-adjust your fingers and slide back one fret to play an A chord.

Next, adjust your fingers once again and slide up one fret from the A to form the D chord once more. Then adjust your fingers one final time, slide back one fret, and form an E chord.

Here is the TAB:

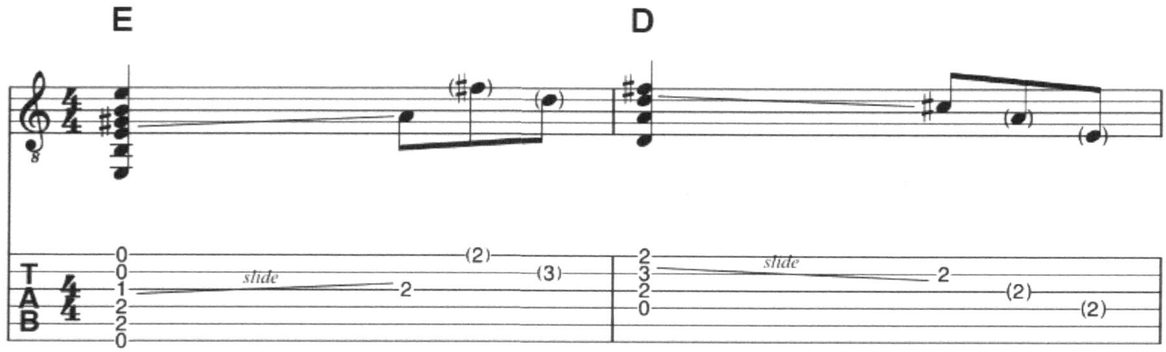

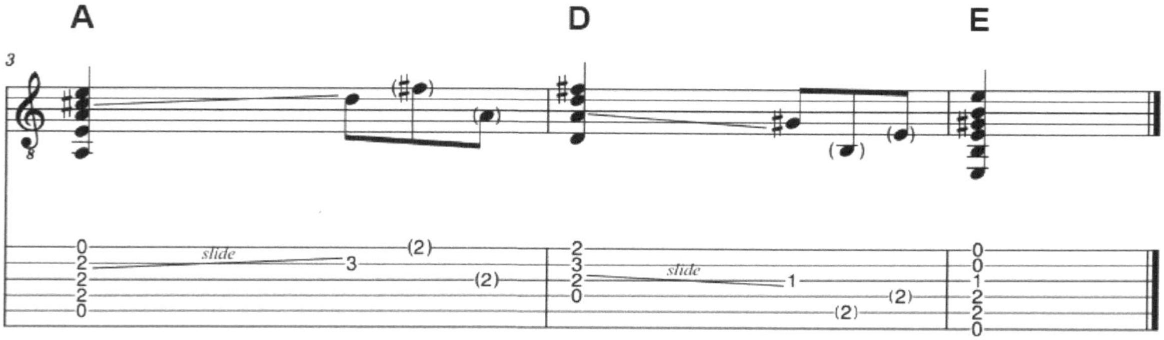

Note: The tablature shows slanted lines across the six TAB lines with the word 'slide' above them. These represent slides, i.e., sliding a finger to a different position on the fretboard. If the line is moving upward, you slide up the neck, or if it's in a downward direction, down the neck.

The numbers in brackets, for example (2), are not played. They represent the frets that you should place your fingers on after completing the slide to create the next chord shape.

To download the audio files for the TAB symbols mentioned in this section, head to **playfirstnote.com/bonuses.**

BONUS CHORDS

The first few chord progressions and songs that we'll be covering only use the A, D, and E chords. However, to fill up your practice schedule and prepare you for the songs that are coming up in later books in this series, here are a few more major chords to practice.

The C Chord

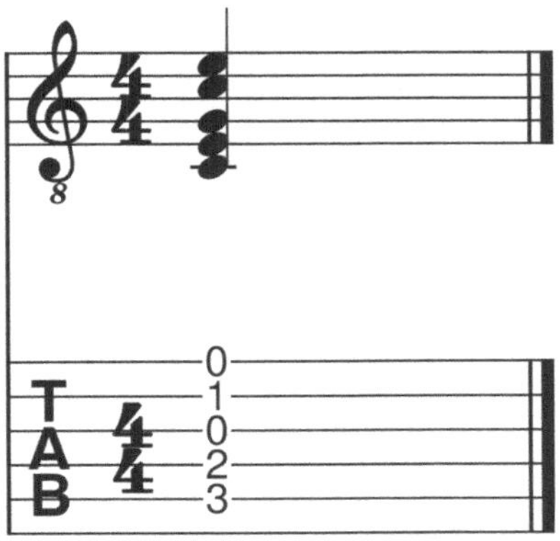

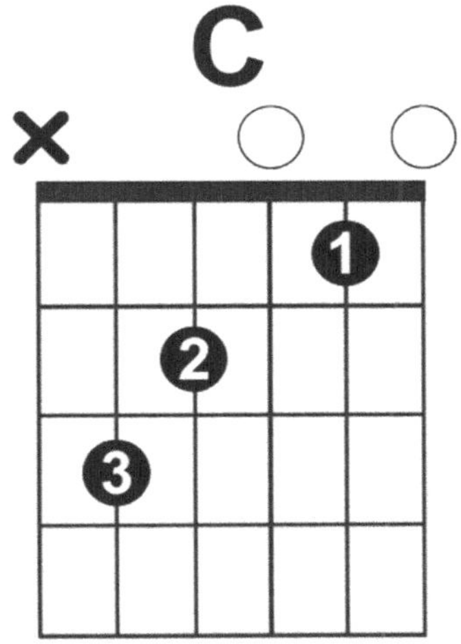

This is, in some ways, easier than some of the chords that we've covered so far because your fingers shouldn't clash with each other. However, it is the first chord we've featured that spans three frets, so there is a bit of a stretch involved.

Start by placing your first finger on the 1st fret of the B string, remembering to position it as close to the fretwire as possible to make the stretch easier. Now put your second finger on the 2nd fret of the D string, and your third finger on the 3rd fret of the A string, as shown below…

Pic 32 - C Chord

As always, give it a strum, then pick the strings. As with the other chords, move your fingers slightly if some of the notes sound muffled.

The G Chord

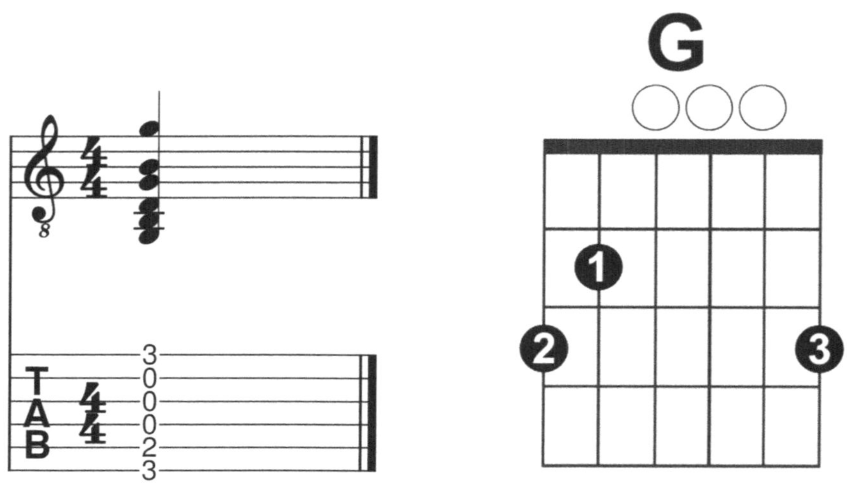

The G chord is also quite a stretch. Start by placing your first finger on the 2nd fret of the A string, then add your second finger on the 3rd fret of the low E string.

So far, so good…

Now you need to place your third finger on the 3rd fret of the high e string, which is where the stretch comes in, as shown below…

Pic 33 - G Chord

There are no real tips or tricks to making this chord comfortable; it's just a case of practice, practice, practice.

And while on the subject of practice, let's have a…

PRACTICE SCHEDULE UPDATE

There's now a lot more that can be added to your daily practice schedule, so let's update it to include all the priceless nuggets of guitar knowledge you've just learned...

	M.M. Speed	Time	M	T	W	T	F
Spider Exercise/Finger Strength	?	3 mins					
Various Melodies	N/A	3 mins					
A, D, & E Chords - Strum & Pick	N/A	3 mins					
1-2-3-4 Chord Change Exercise	N/A	3 mins					
Any Chord - Adjust until perfect	N/A	2 mins					
Quick Change Chord Exercise	N/A	3 mins					
C and G Chords - Strum & Pick	N/A	3 mins					

To download a blank printable PDF version of the weekly practice schedule, please visit **playfirstnote.com/bonuses.**

Practice Notes

- Because there is more to practice now, I've reduced the number of exercises to one per day, alternating between Spider on one day and one of the Finger Strength exercises on the next. The Metronome speed setting, which is shown as a '?' in the diagram, will be dictated by how quickly you are playing them, so insert your current speed.
- If you're using a metronome, don't put a check mark in the checkbox as you do for the other exercises; put the speed you played at on a particular day, then you can instantly see your progress.
- For 'Various Melodies', you can alternate between them until you're happy with how they all sound. If you're finding one harder than the others, concentrate on practising that.
- In case you're confused, 'Any Chord - Adjust until perfect' is perfecting every note of a chord by starting with one finger, getting it clear, then adding another finger, etc. You can use any chord you are having problems with.

Everyone learns things in their own way and at their own pace. Some people find melodies easy while others struggle with them. Some make their chords sound good in a few hours, others might take three or four days.

It's impossible for me to analyze your playing, so adapt the Practice Schedule to your requirements. If you need to spend more time perfecting the melodies, add them back to your daily schedule. Or, if you can already play them all perfectly, remove them and concentrate on the chords.

Now that we have some great-sounding chords, let's put them all together and play some songs…

CHAPTER 5
IT'S ALL IN THE RHYTHM
YOUR GUIDE TO STRUMMING PATTERNS, TIME SIGNATURES, AND GROOVES

It's time to get rhythmical, so get that strumming arm ready for action, because once it gets going, there's no stopping it.

The majority of songs that feature a guitar will have some type of strumming. It might be the riffs, solos, and other fancy guitar tricks that catch your ear, but underneath all the glitter, you will normally find guitars glueing the song together with a rhythm pattern or two.

However, some songs, such as "What's Up" by the Four Non Blondes, have less guitar bling and are built on a strong rhythm pattern that doesn't change for nearly the whole length of the song.

But what are rhythm patterns? Well, let's get straight to it with Music Theory Snippet #4 to find out...

What is a Rhythm Pattern?

Rhythm patterns are the rhythmic patterns - no real surprise there! - that are played in a song and usually fill one bar of music. They usually repeat themselves for a whole section, such as a verse or chorus, or may even remain the same throughout the whole song.

Even though a song has a rhythm pattern, a guitarist (or any other musician) might vary it slightly throughout the song, this may involve using dynamics, i.e., playing it quieter or louder during certain sections, or by playing it more minimally in quieter parts of a song, such as the verse.

However, there's another important thing we need to mention before we can play the rhythm patterns properly, Music Theory Snippet #5...

What is a Time Signature?

Time signatures can be quite complex, so I'll be covering them in more detail in future books in this series.

But, for now. A time signature is an indication of time and rhythm. They are indicated as a fraction, with the top number showing the number of beats in a bar and the lower number representing the length of each beat, for example, 3/4 or 4/4.

I know that sounds very complicated, so here's a simpler explanation.

I'm sure that when you listen to music, you have noticed that most songs contain bars that have four beats in them. You may also have heard musicians, particularly drummers, start songs when playing live by either counting 1-2-3-4 on their drumsticks or even saying the numbers into a microphone; punk pioneers, The Ramones, were particularly famed for starting nearly every song with a slurred 1-2-3-4.

This represents the four beats in each bar of the song they are going to play. And the speed at which they play or say "1-2-3-4" represents how quickly the song will be played.

Therefore, the time signature 4/4 represents 4 beats, all of which are a quarter note in length - 1-2-3-4. While a 3/4 time signature represents 3 beats per bar, again, each one is a quarter note in length - 1-2-3.

Pro Tip: You can remember the feel and timing of a 3/4 time signature by thinking of a waltz, 1-2-3, 1-2-3, 1-2-3, etc.

Let's start with the most basic 3/4 rhythm pattern...

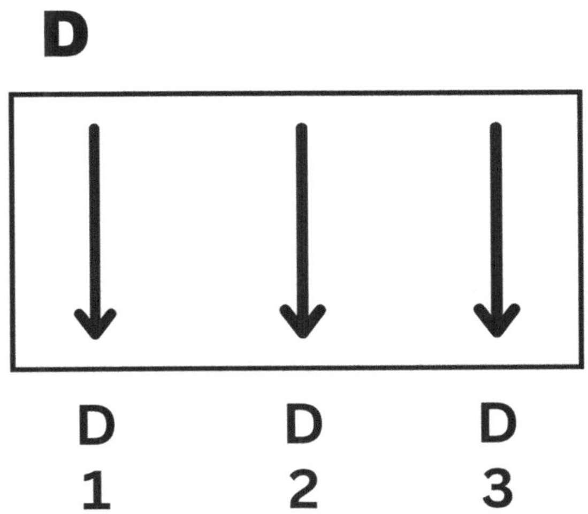

As you can see, this is one bar of music, containing three downstrokes, the first on the count of '1', the next on the count of '2', and the final downstroke on the count of '3'.

Let's try a little exercise: Play a D chord and count 1-2-3 out loud continually while playing a downstroke on every beat. Nice, sounds good, doesn't it, but it doesn't really sound much like a song. Don't worry, it will very, very soon.

Now change the chord to one of the others that you know and play the rhythm again for a few minutes.

But where does the beat start?

That's a great question, and you're right, it does all sound the same, just down, down, down, continually. So, let's play it slightly differently.

Instead of strumming every beat with the same strength of strum, play the downstroke on the '1' count a little harder, as shown below…

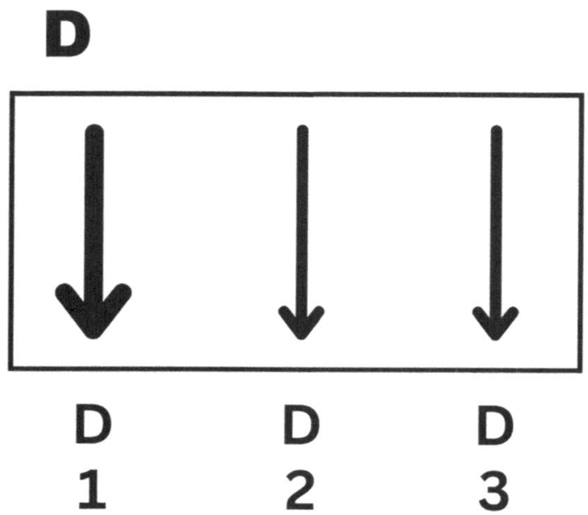

That sounds a lot better. Now you can tell where every bar starts and finishes, excellent.

The final part of the puzzle

We are now going to add one more strum, and this is where the magic really happens; it's actually hard to believe that adding a simple upstroke can make this much difference.

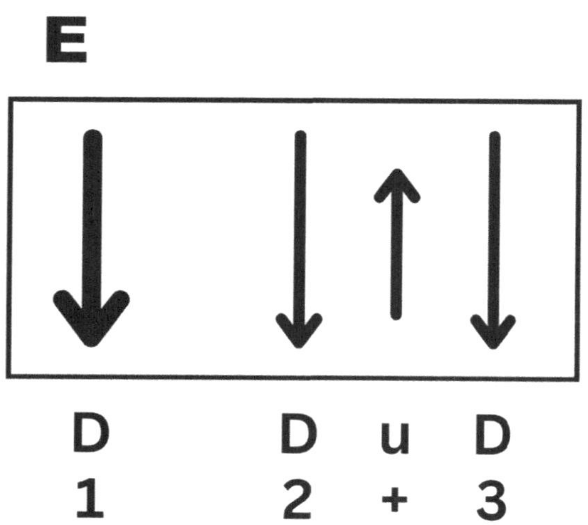

The upstroke is played exactly halfway between the second downstroke and the third. This really is the icing on the cake. The boring old repetitive downstroke rhythm now sounds like the songs you listen to every day.

Let's do the same with a 4/4 rhythm pattern, but in a little less detail...

Basic 4/4 Rhythm

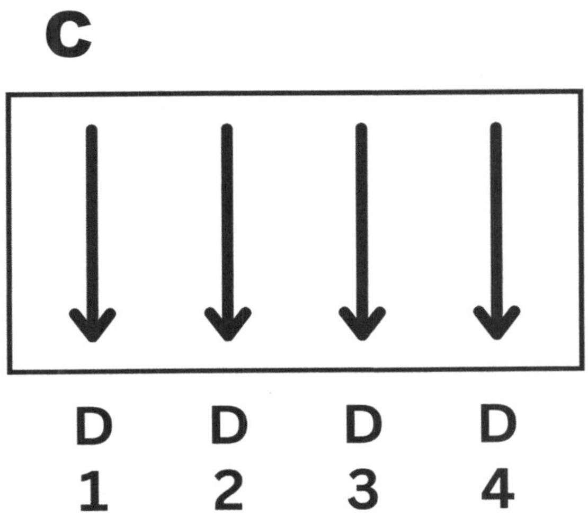

Now let's emphasize the first note…

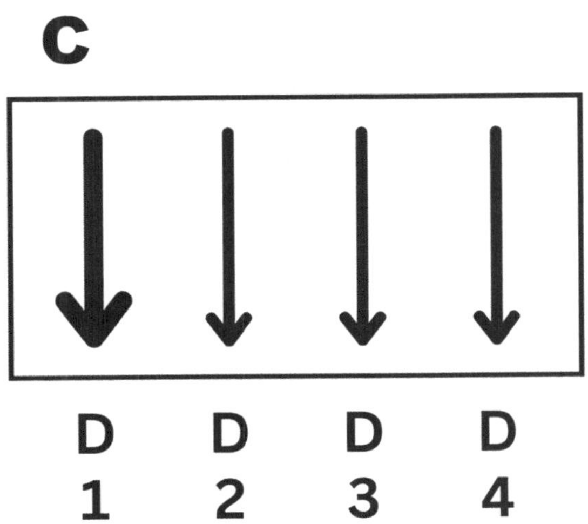

And let's add the all-important upstroke, but this time it's halfway between the third and fourth downstrokes…

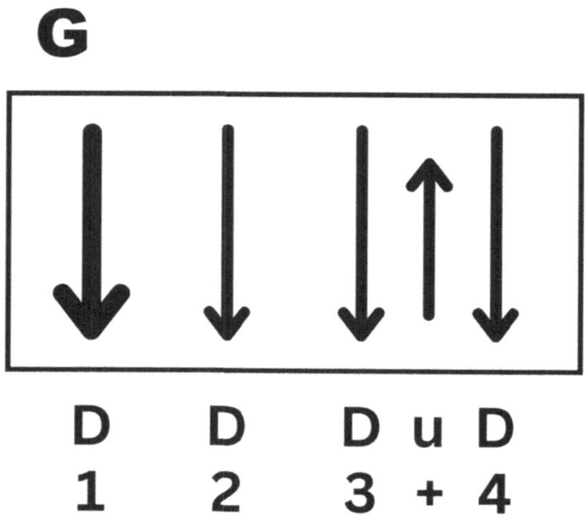

It's now time for some chord progressions so that we can change the chords around a bit while you're mastering the different rhythm patterns.

CHORD PROGRESSION 1 - 3/4

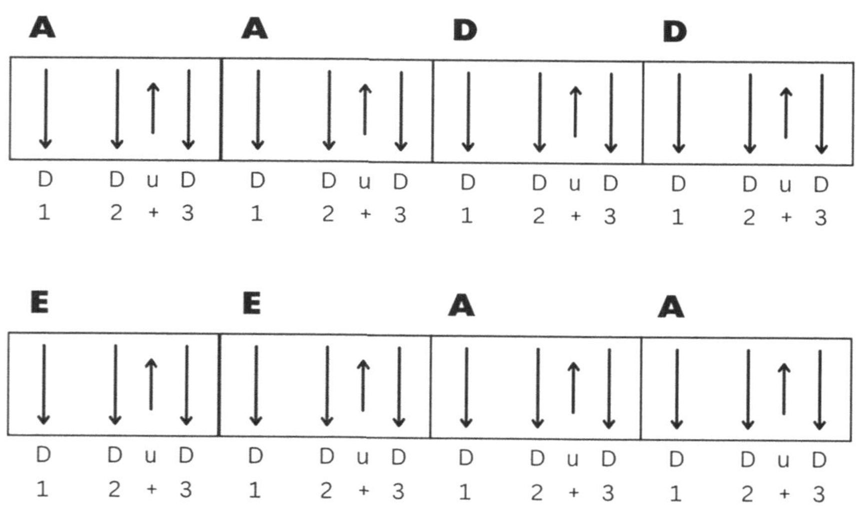

This should be easy enough to play. Start with two bars of the A chord, playing the fun 1-2+3 rhythm we just learned. Then change to a D chord for two bars, then to an E chord for another two, then end with two bars of A, again playing the same rhythm.

To download the audio files for the chord progressions mentioned in this section, head to **playfirstnote.com/bonuses.**

CHORD PROGRESSION 2 - 3/4

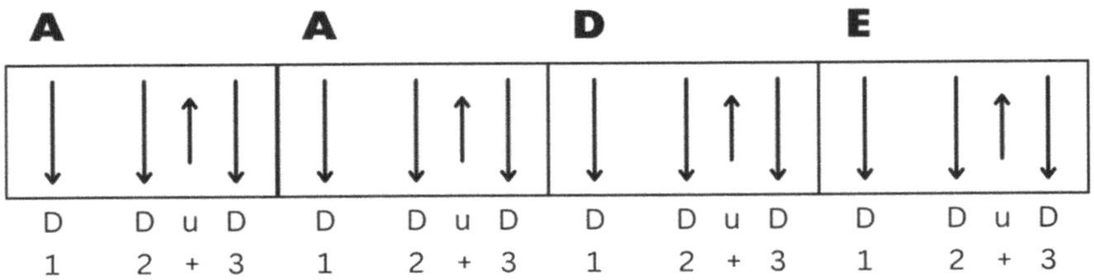

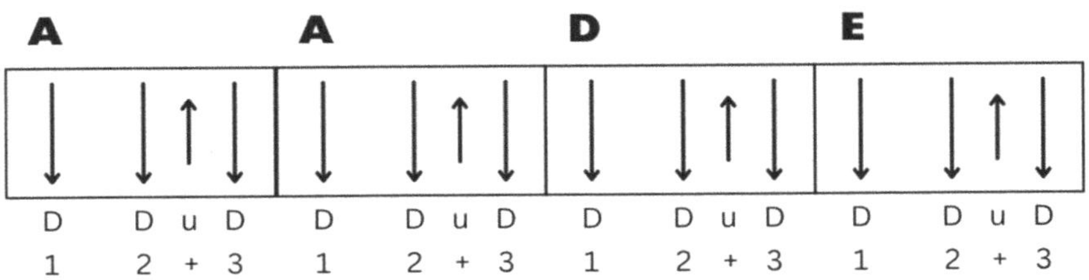

This starts in the same way as the first progression, then you only play one bar of D, followed by a bar of E, before repeating the sequence.

CHORD PROGRESSION 3 - 4/4

E	E	D	D
↓ ↓ ↓↑↓	↓ ↓ ↓↑↓	↓ ↓ ↓↑↓	↓ ↓ ↓↑↓
D D D u D	D D D u D	D D D u D	D D D u D
1 2 3 + 4	1 2 3 + 4	1 2 3 + 4	1 2 3 + 4

A	A	D	D
↓ ↓ ↓↑↓	↓ ↓ ↓↑↓	↓ ↓ ↓↑↓	↓ ↓ ↓↑↓
D D D u D	D D D u D	D D D u D	D D D u D
1 2 3 + 4	1 2 3 + 4	1 2 3 + 4	1 2 3 + 4

Let's change the rhythm to 4/4. The chords should be simple enough - two Es, two Ds, two As, ending with a pair of Ds.

CHORD PROGRESSION 4 - 4/4

E	D	E	E
↓ ↓ ↓↑↓	↓ ↓ ↓↑↓	↓ ↓ ↓↑↓	↓ ↓ ↓↑↓
D D D u D	D D D u D	D D D u D	D D D u D
1 2 3 + 4	1 2 3 + 4	1 2 3 + 4	1 2 3 + 4

D	A	E	D
↓ ↓ ↓↑↓	↓ ↓ ↓↑↓	↓ ↓ ↓↑↓	↓ ↓ ↓↑↓
D D D u D	D D D u D	D D D u D	D D D u D
1 2 3 + 4	1 2 3 + 4	1 2 3 + 4	1 2 3 + 4

Let's mix it up for the final progression. We'll stay in 4/4 but add a few more chord changes.

Start with an E for one bar, before moving to a D, and going back to the E for bars 3 and 4. For bar 5, go back to D, then to A, then to E, finishing with a D.

THE IMPORTANCE OF PLAYING ALONG

I know that your chords don't sound great yet, and that your chord changes could be much quicker. But the next point is so important that I'm going to start drilling it into your head at this early stage…

Play along with music as much as you can!

I know that you think it's impossible, but that isn't the case. You won't be able to put a YouTube video on and play along with it; that's way too difficult, plus, you don't even know any songs yet!

However, there are other things you can play along with, for example, metronomes. But they can be a bit boring to play rhythm patterns with because the endless tick-tock, even though it's great for exercises, gets a bit tedious when playing a rhythm.

So replace them with something more interesting, such as a drum machine, a beats app, or online drum patterns.

Drum machines are fantastic; they can either be dedicated, i.e., they can only be used to make and play beats. Or they can be part of another instrument, for example, a lot of digital keyboards, even the small, cheap ones, contain some interesting drum rhythms.

Or, if you want a free option, either download an app that features drumbeats or loops, or go online and search for drum patterns/beats. There are countless options, and many allow you to vary the timing, i.e., slow the beat down or speed it up.

Whatever option you choose, find a rhythm you enjoy playing with and set it to a slow speed that you can strum along to while just about managing to keep the chord changes going. As every day passes, it will get easier and easier, so you can continually increase the speed a little.

Playing along with Recordings

As you improve, try playing along with the actual recording. You can use YouTube, Spotify, or wherever you stream your music, or if you're more old school, play along with records or CDs.

It will be difficult at first, and you'll constantly lose your place, but don't worry, just wait till the beginning of the next line or even till the start of the next chorus, verse, or whatever.

Over time, and with lots of practice, it will get easier and easier, until one day, you will be playing your favorite songs from start to finish. You can then go one step further and learn whole albums or live concerts.

Here's an embarrassing story from my youth to end this chapter...

I was a huge fan of The Cult in my early teens and learnt nearly every song they released from start to finish. I did it because I loved their music.

However, when they started releasing VHS videos of live concerts (yes, it was a while ago, before the time of DVDs), I would learn those as well. Most of the songs were the same or very similar to those on the records, so not a great deal of extra work.

But... one day, while I was halfway through playing one of their live concert videos, it hit me - if I'm in the crowd about to watch the band live and the singer comes on stage to apologize that there will be no show tonight because the guitarist has sprained his finger. I would shout out...

"No worries, I'll play, I know the songs, I even know the setlist!"

In my dreams, I would then get up on stage and shock the band and the audience with my amazing six-string skills and become the guitar hero I was destined to be.

Unsurprisingly, it never happened; the guitarist was always fit and well in every Cult gig I ever went to, so I never had my chance. But knowing that I could have done it gave me a lot of confidence when I was playing in bands.

On a side note: The singer of a band I was playing session guitar for arranged for Billy Duffy, the Cult's guitarist, to join us on stage to play one of the Cult's hits, many, many years later.

We played "She Sells Sanctuary"; he played lead, I played rhythm. After the show, I told him the story I just told you - he laughed out loud and walked off. I haven't seen him since…

BACK TO THE PLOT…

…for one more MASSIVE gain from playing along with songs you love. When it's time to form or join a band, you'll have a much easier time than someone who wasn't a play-along junkie.

As the drummer starts the song (they usually do in band practice), all you have to do is play the exact same parts that you've been playing along with the recording or a live concert.

As long as everyone else in the band has learned their parts properly, you should all make your way through the song with no epic fails.

You've already played all the songs countless times with some of the best drummers, bassists, keyboard players, and singers in the world - on the recordings - so, playing with some local musicians should be a breeze, as long as they are up to the task.

This not only calms your nerves when playing and jamming with other musicians but also gives you confidence in your abilities, which will turn you into a better guitarist and performer.

That's enough stories and motivation for one chapter, so let's get to the next one, where we'll start learning some songs.

CHAPTER 6
PUTTING THE CHORDS TOGETHER
PLAYING SONGS

Now that you've got the hang of playing a few chords and know some rhythm patterns in both 3/4 and 4/4, let's use them to create the most important thing in music - songs!

Songs are simply a series of chords played in a particular time using a certain rhythm. I know that's quite hard to believe when you think of your favorites - songs that can make you smile or cry - but in their most basic form, that really is all they are.

Obviously, genius songwriters and composers know which chords to use, and in what order, to create the emotion they are trying to express. They also know the perfect melody to sing or play over them to pull the heartstrings or make you want to get up and dance. But, once again, they are just a series of chords.

And guess what? You know three chords, five if you include the C and the G! So, let's use them to play some songs.

However...

You might be thinking that it can't be easy to find a song that only has three chords in it? Well, you couldn't be further from the truth. There are thousands of songs that only contain three chords, and luckily for us, a lot of them include A, D, and E.

We'll start with one of the most famous songs in the world, which is sung in countless countries in a variety of languages.

This makes it a great first choice, because I'm sure you know it well. You probably don't listen to it that often, let's be honest, the latest rock and pop songs are far better, but to get us going on our journey, it's perfect, the song is...

AMAZING GRACE - 3/4

A				A				D				A			
↓	↓	↑	↓	↓	↓	↑	↓	↓	↓	↑	↓	↓	↓	↑	↓
D	D	u	D	D	D	u	D	D	D	u	D	D	D	u	D
1	2	+	3	1	2	+	3	1	2	+	3	1	2	+	3

A				A				E				E			
↓	↓	↑	↓	↓	↓	↑	↓	↓	↓	↑	↓	↓	↓	↑	↓
D	D	u	D	D	D	u	D	D	D	u	D	D	D	u	D
1	2	+	3	1	2	+	3	1	2	+	3	1	2	+	3

A				A				D				A			
↓	↓	↑	↓	↓	↓	↑	↓	↓	↓	↑	↓	↓	↓	↑	↓
D	D	u	D	D	D	u	D	D	D	u	D	D	D	u	D
1	2	+	3	1	2	+	3	1	2	+	3	1	2	+	3

A				E				A				A			
↓	↓	↑	↓	↓	↓	↑	↓	↓	↓	↑	↓	↓	↓	↑	↓
D	D	u	D	D	D	u	D	D	D	u	D	D	D	u	D
1	2	+	3	1	2	+	3	1	2	+	3	1	2	+	3

That looks simple enough, doesn't it? Surprisingly simple, to be perfectly honest.

You already know the three chords - A - D - E - and you can play the basic 3/4 rhythm of the song. Plus, we've already covered lots of these progressions at the end of the last chapter, so you've already played most of this song, just not all at once.

However, your chord changes are still probably too slow to make it sound like a 'song'. Unfortunately, there is no way around this; I've already shown you the anchor notes on the same string trick to make the changes easier.

So, it's just a case of practice, practice, practice, until the changes get smoother and quicker.

Don't worry, it shouldn't take too long, and you'll be strumming your way through this and the other songs in no time.

To download the audio files for the songs featured in this section, head to **playfirstnote.com/bonuses.**

But it doesn't sound like Amazing Grace?

Pupils often say this after they've been playing it for a while. They don't see a connection between the words of the song and the chords.

This is completely normal and is mainly due to the fact that 98% of your brain is concentrating on remembering the chords, getting the rhythm in time, and worrying about the next chord change. The other 2% is concentrating on breathing to keep you alive!

Singing while playing is a whole new level of difficulty for beginners. As I said, if 98% of your brain is concentrating on playing the song, you only have 2% left. If you use that to sing, you'll forget to breathe—not a good thing!!!

In order to start singing, your playing needs to become more natural. As you start to use a smaller percentage of your brain power to play, you can use it to concentrate on singing. Then the song starts to make sense.

Here is the song again, but with the words included...

A	A	D	A
↓ ↓ ↑ ↓	↓ ↓ ↑ ↓	↓ ↓ ↑ ↓	↓ ↓ ↑ ↓
D D u D	D D u D	D D u D	D D u D
1 2 + 3	1 2 + 3	1 2 + 3	1 2 + 3
-ma------------zing	gra----ce how	sw-e-e-t the	so-u-nd that

A	A	E	E
↓ ↓ ↑ ↓	↓ ↓ ↑ ↓	↓ ↓ ↑ ↓	↓ ↓ ↑ ↓
D D u D	D D u D	D D u D	D D u D
1 2 + 3	1 2 + 3	1 2 + 3	1 2 + 3
sa-v-ed a	wretch like	me	I

A	A	D	A
↓ ↓ ↑ ↓	↓ ↓ ↑ ↓	↓ ↓ ↑ ↓	↓ ↓ ↑ ↓
D D u D	D D u D	D D u D	D D u D
1 2 + 3	1 2 + 3	1 2 + 3	1 2 + 3
on----ce was	lost but	now am	found was

A	E	A	A
↓ ↓ ↑ ↓	↓ ↓ ↑ ↓	↓ ↓ ↑ ↓	↓ ↓ ↑ ↓
D D u D	D D u D	D D u D	D D u D
1 2 + 3	1 2 + 3	1 2 + 3	1 2 + 3
bli----nd but	now I	se-----e	

Note: You'll notice that the first word is '-mazing', not 'Amazing', this is because the 'A-' is sung before starting to play the first bar of the song.

This version of the song makes it a lot easier to understand how the words and the chords fit together, but better still, let's learn another melody…

Amazing Grace Melody

A A D
A A A E
E A A D
A A E A

You now have the choice of either singing it or playing it, or better still, record yourself playing the chords on your smartphone or laptop, then play the melody over it. You'll be a recording pro in no time!

Congratulations, you've just learned your first song. Admittedly, it's not the greatest song ever written, so don't worry, we'll get to them, but we have to start somewhere.

Practice it from start to finish as many times as you like. Perfecting this song will make every new one we learn easier from now on.

So, where do we go from here?

Another song, obviously, how about one in 4/4 that we've already learned the melody for…

LONDON BRIDGE IS FALLING DOWN - 4/4

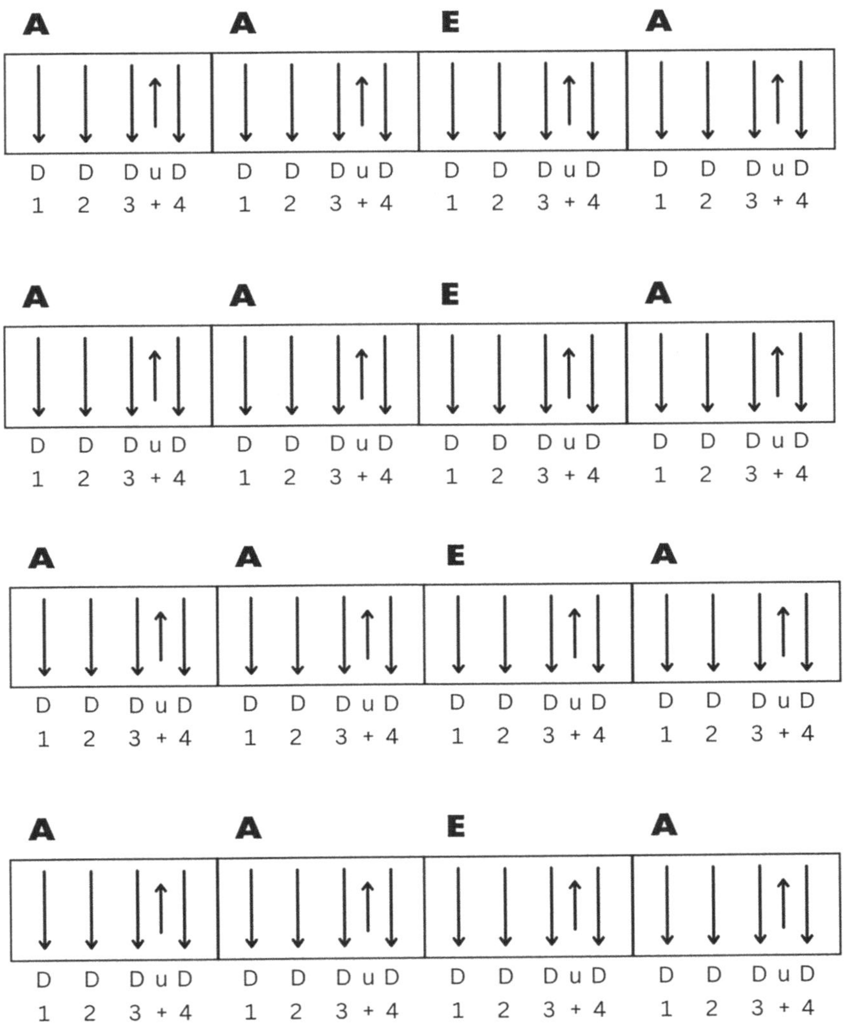

Time for our second rhythm, a 4/4, which shouldn't cause you any problems if you've been practising the chord progressions at the end of the last chapter.

And to make up for the fact that you've got to play a D D DuD rhythm, instead of the slightly easier D DuD we used in Amazing Grace, there are only two chords to play in this song.

Yes, that's right, only an A chord and an E chord. It couldn't get much simpler. Follow it through playing a 4/4 rhythm in every box/bar.

Here's the song again, but with the words...

A	A	E	A

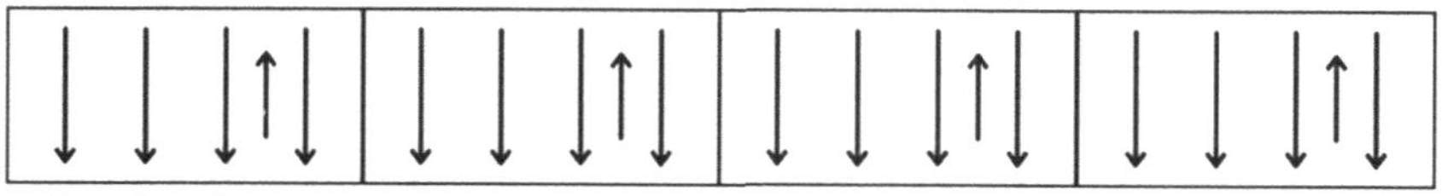

D D D u D	D D D u D	D D D u D	D D D u D
1 2 3 + 4	1 2 3 + 4	1 2 3 + 4	1 2 3 + 4
London Bridge is	fall-ing down	fall-ing down	fall-ing down

A	A	E	A

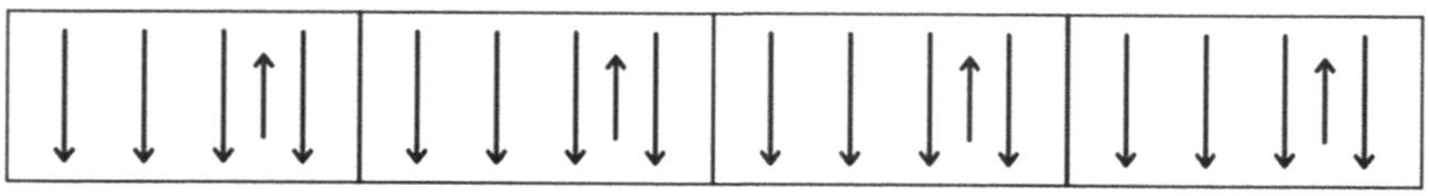

D D D u D	D D D u D	D D D u D	D D D u D
1 2 3 + 4	1 2 3 + 4	1 2 3 + 4	1 2 3 + 4
London Bridge is	fall-ing down	my fair	la---dy

A	A	E	A

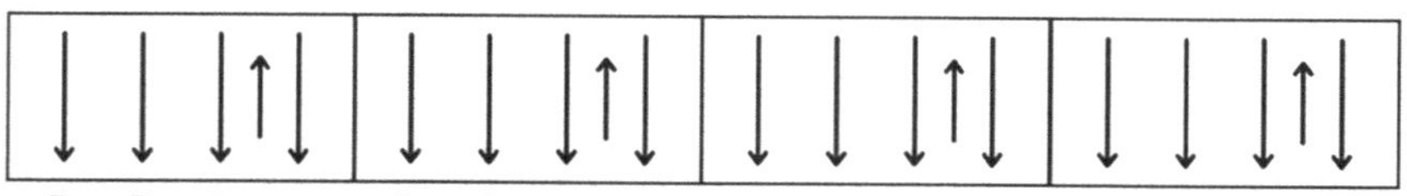

D D D u D	D D D u D	D D D u D	D D D u D
1 2 3 + 4	1 2 3 + 4	1 2 3 + 4	1 2 3 + 4
Build it up with	iron and steel	iron and steel	iron and steel

A	A	E	A

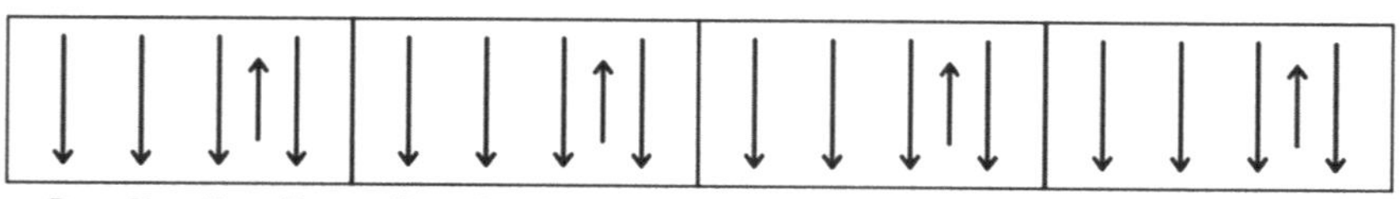

D D D u D	D D D u D	D D D u D	D D D u D
1 2 3 + 4	1 2 3 + 4	1 2 3 + 4	1 2 3 + 4
Build it up with	iron and steel	my fair	la---dy

And here is the melody once more, if you want to record yourself, and then play over it. Or if you have a guitar-playing friend, get them involved, and you can have a jam!

Now we're talking!!!

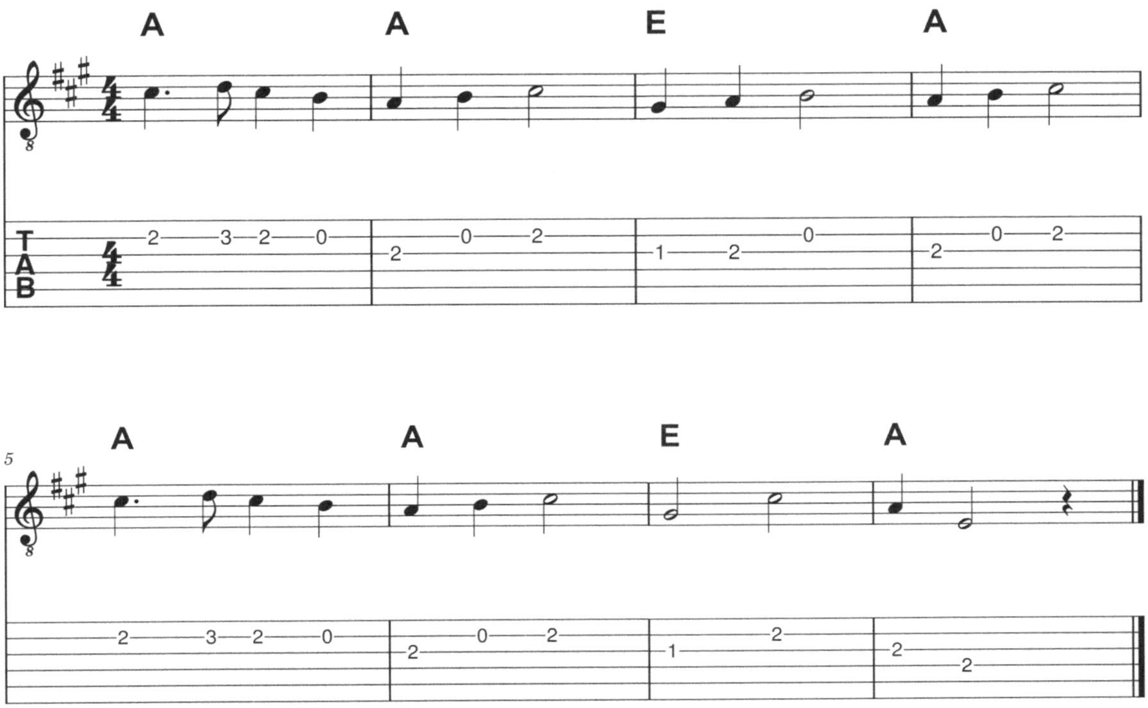

Two songs down, one more to go, this time we'll go back to the 3/4 rhythm to play…

HAPPY BIRTHDAY 3/4

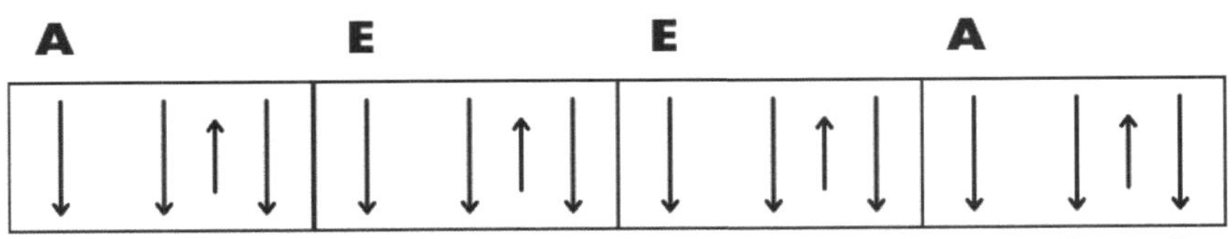

D D u D D D u D D D u D D D u D

1 2 + 3 1 2 + 3 1 2 + 3 1 2 + 3

Birth--day to you, Happy Birth--day to you, Happy

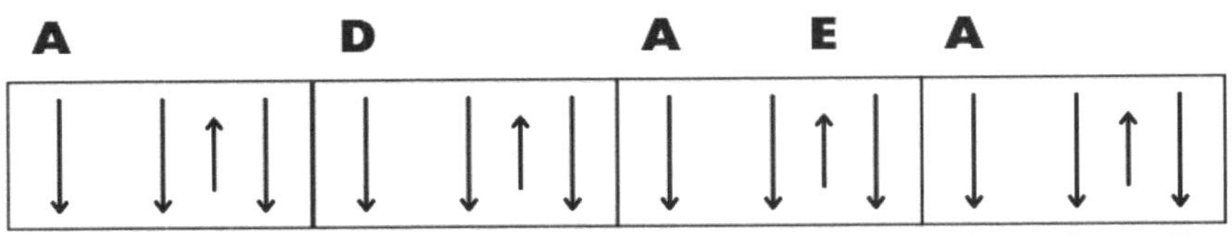

D D u D D D u D D D u D D D u D

1 2 + 3 1 2 + 3 1 2 + 3 1 2 + 3

Birth--day Dear Some-one Happy Birth--day to you, Happy

Sticking with the same 3/4 rhythm, let's celebrate a birthday!

Same chords, same rhythm, so once again, it shouldn't be that difficult.

However, Bar 7 might be a little tricky because you have to play two different chords, not the usual one in the same bar. The rhythm pattern is exactly the same as the one used in every other bar, but you need to change chords halfway through it.

To do this, play the first two downstrokes on the A chord, then change to an E chord for the upstroke and the final downstroke.

It's tough when you first try it, not just remembering where to change, but also changing chords fast enough to keep the rhythm - and the song - going, but it will get easier soon.

Play it really slowly at first, trying to keep the beat, then, as with everything else we've covered, speed up slowly as you improve.

And here's the melody, so you've got even more to practice...

Wow, you can now play three different songs - FANTASTIC!

You'll be a true rockstar in no time at all! In fact, you've already got three songs for the setlist of your first concert (but the song choice might need some slightly more upbeat numbers, come to think of it).

Regardless, you're well on your way. The songs probably don't sound great yet, but they should be getting better every day as your fingers get used to the positions, your strumming improves, and your chord changes get quicker.

Keep practising all the songs, over and over again, until you get comfortable playing them.

And have a go at singing along if you can; the sooner you start, the better. Plus, it will actually improve your playing because concentrating on singing will make your chord changes and strumming more natural.

CHAPTER 7
COMMON MISTAKES
THE PITFALLS EVERY NEW GUITARIST FACES AND HOW TO FIX THEM

Hopefully, the melodies and the songs we've learned together are sounding good. Your chords sound nice and clear most of the time, and your rhythm patterns are, well… rhythmic!

You can also play through the songs without a massive dose of the sound of silence between every chord, and when you play any of the melodies, your friends and family can easily recognize them.

In a perfect world, that would most definitely be the case, but unfortunately, for lots of beginners, it sadly isn't. So what's gone wrong, and why don't things sound the way you'd like them to?

Well, that's what we'll be finding out in this chapter, starting with…

UNREALISTIC EXPECTATIONS

This is by far the most common problem beginners have, especially when they are not regularly interacting with a good teacher or better guitarists. You have no idea how good you should be at this stage.

However, neither I nor a good teacher could actually answer that question because there are so many factors involved.

We all learn differently and at our own pace, and since playing guitar is both a mental and physical skill, your brain might know exactly what you should be doing, but your hands and fingers don't want to get involved.

This can be very frustrating because you're looking at the hands that have been with you since birth, and now, all of a sudden, they have become arrogant teenagers who don't want to listen to you anymore.

On top of that, only you know how many hours you have practised up until this stage, and if you were completely focused while doing it, or were you checking your phone every few minutes?

This makes such a difference, and I know how hard it is to get into the habit of sitting down and only focusing on your guitar playing for 20 minutes five days a week. But to become a good, great, or even exceptional guitarist, you have to do it.

As an experiment, check your daily screentime report on your smartphone; it's probably in the hours, possibly a lot of them! So, how about watching fewer cat videos and spending a little bit more time on becoming a guitar legend! It's well worth the effort.

I'M NOT A PERFECTIONIST

That's not a huge problem, plus, you don't have to be a perfectionist to try and achieve perfection. I'm sure that even if you don't think you are one, there are lots of perfect things in your life that you wouldn't want any other way.

Trying to achieve perfection will really help you on your guitar-playing journey. It might seem like it's the slow path, but, in fact, it's the opposite.

Spending ages slightly moving each finger to make every note in a chord ring out is incredibly boring. I know, I spent hours/days/weeks doing it myself, many years ago. But when you get a few chords sounding great, all the new chords you learn will quickly follow suit.

However, if you carry on playing muffled, bad-sounding chords, you'll start to accept that as normal, and everything you play will sound a bit off. Your playing won't be enjoyable to listen to, and you may well give up altogether.

Therefore, be patient and work on getting your chords to sound perfect now. All the time you spend, and so much more, will be freed up in the future when you instantly play new and far harder chords without even thinking about it.

I DON'T THINK I'M A NATURAL; PLAYING GUITAR SEEMS VERY DIFFICULT

I constantly hear this from beginners, and it's complete rubbish.

Do you think that Jimi Hendrix, Jimmy Page, Eddie Van Halen, Randy Rhoads, Zack Wylde, Slash, John Mayer, or '..................' [insert your personal guitar hero] picked up a guitar for the first time and could magically play the solo to their favorite song perfectly?

Of course not, what they did was learn a few basic chords, such as A, D, E, C, and G, and a few rhythm patterns, then put it all together to play a few songs. They also probably had a go at a few simple melodies.

And guess what, you have just learned exactly the same things that your heroes did. And I assure you that at this stage of their development, they probably sounded very similar to how you sound today.

So, what's the difference between you and your heroes?

At this stage, absolutely nothing. The only difference is that 'at this stage' to them was 10, 20, 30, 40, 50, or even 60 years ago.

Over that time, they have practised, and practised, and practised, to perfect their art. They have written songs, played concerts, recorded countless albums/CDs, played on TV, appeared on the covers of guitar magazines, etc., etc.

And there is nothing stopping you from following the exact same path. Regardless of how old you are now, it's all down to practising and pursuing the dream.

If you want to play live - form or join a band, if you want to record a song - start writing one, or if all you've ever wanted to do is sing and play some songs around the barbecue to entertain your family and friends - learn some sing-along songs.

Nothing is stopping you from achieving anything, apart from yourself. So get into the habit of daily 20-minute practice routines; they really are the key to your success.

BUT MY FINGERS HURT SO BAD

This varies greatly from one player to the next. Some feel next to no pain, either from their fingertips when pressing down on thin pieces of wire or from stretching and contorting their fingers into ridiculous positions.

Others, however, do suffer from it, so here is my advice…

If you allow your calluses to develop slowly, they should not become painful, which is why the 20-minute-per-day routine with two days off works so well.

Usually, if your fingertips hurt, it's because you are practising too much, i.e., more than the recommended 20 minutes. This could be because you're an absolute guitar freak and just can't get enough - if so, I praise you!

However, the main reason that lots of beginners practice for longer than they should is to make up for lost time. Taking three days off and then doing an hour's practice in one session isn't good for your fingertips or your advancement as a musician.

So, try to stick to the 20-minute sessions, and make sure that the two days you take off per week are spaced out, so that your fingertips have time to rest.

I know that due to work and family pressures, this isn't always possible. If this is the case, make sure to split multiple sessions over, for example, the weekend, into a maximum of 20 minutes, leaving at least four to five hours between each one to rest your fingertips.

Also, never practice after a warm bath or shower, or after you've been swimming. Your fingertips will be soft and much more likely to become painful.

I'll end this chapter with another little story…

I played in a band with a bassist who went on to become one of London's top session players many years ago. He was an absolute beast of a musician and could outplay nearly anyone on a bass.

We were in the same band for about three years, and most of the time our schedule wasn't that hectic, but occasionally it was.

The band coped quite well; the other guitarist and I both played Gibson Les Pauls, which can get heavy on the shoulders playing long sets night after night, and the singer had to rest his voice every few days, which is normal. The drummer had no issues at all.

But the bassist occasionally had problems with the fingertips on his non-fretting hand, the one he used to play the strings. He only played fingerstyle bass and played hard.

The reason I'm recounting this tale is that even though he had practised for countless years, developed calluses, and knew how to play his instrument better than most, even he occasionally had issues with fingertip pain.

So, if you do get pain in your fingertips, you've probably been overdoing things, so rest for a few days, and the pain should go away.

BTW: His solution, and this is in no way recommended, was superglue. He used to put it on his fingertips to get through gigs - nasty!

CHAPTER 8
NEXT STEPS
KEEP ROCKING THE GUITAR

Wow, we've made it to the final chapter, and what a journey it's been. You started as a complete guitar rookie, and you've worked through knowing every part of a guitar and how to hold it, as well as how to hold a pick, strum, and play notes. You now understand how to read tablature, can play a variety of different melodies, and three complete songs.

Along the way, you've learned the most important major chords, some exercises to get your fingers moving more efficiently and effectively, the best ways to practice, a little bit of music theory, and lots of other information that will prove invaluable to any bona fide rockstar!

You're well on your way now - own it!

SO, WHAT'S NEXT?

Even though some, if not most, of the melodies and songs I've included in this book are a bit basic and more than likely not what you dream of playing on a guitar, it's for a reason. It would be great to start with Guns N' Roses, Nirvana, Metallica, Led Zeppelin, Green Day, Linkin Park, Red Hot Chili Peppers, or your favorite band's songs and melodies, but unfortunately, they don't have any songs that only contain A, D, and E, and use a simple repeating rhythm.

However, don't worry, Book 2 and later books in this series feature songs, riffs, licks, and solos by these and all your other favorite bands.

Going from a complete beginner to playing like one of your guitar heroes is a step-by-step journey. It can't be rushed; you have to create a foundation that you can build your guitar skills on, and once you've mastered everything included in this book, you will have the most solid foundation possible.

So, the next step is to practice, practice, practice, everything in this book until it becomes second nature. Don't worry about the fact that you don't really like "London Bridge Is Falling Down". It's there to take you to the next level; it's a stepping stone to playing the songs you love. So practice it until you can play it perfectly. The chords in the song are also in the ones you want to play, which will also feature variations on the rhythm, plus being able to play the notes in the melody effortlessly will come in useful when you start learning licks and your favorite solos.

Step by step, and very soon, these basic songs and melodies will give you the foundation that will enable you to play more complex songs by the greatest bands of all time with ease. And that's exactly what we'll be covering in…

GUITAR ROOKIE TO ROCKSTAR BOOK 2

There's lots to look forward to in the next instalment, where we'll take everything you've learnt so far up a notch. There'll be loads more songs, again featuring A, D, and E, as well as C and G, and also introducing your first three minor chords - Am, Dm, and Em. We'll also be covering some more complex rhythm patterns as well as taking a look at pick and fingerpicking techniques.

Plus, we'll learn how to play riffs and scales as we start looking at the super fun side of being a musician - lead guitar techniques.

The guitar world's your oyster! You're well on your way to becoming the rockstar you've always dreamt of being, so keep on rocking the 20 minutes of focused practice every day, and very soon, your guitar wizardry will shine through.

Looking forward to catching up again in Book 2…

ACKNOWLEDGMENT

To every new guitarist who shared their struggles, breakthroughs, and excitement - thank you.

Your questions, dedication, and passion shaped this book far more than you know. To my family and friends, your endless patience and encouragement kept this project moving, one chapter at a time. Thank you for believing in this mission as much as I do.

And to the team at FirstNote, your creativity, feedback, and attention to detail helped transform Guitar Rookie to Rockstar – Book 1 into a clear, practical roadmap for beginners taking their very first steps toward becoming confident guitarists.

ABOUT THE AUTHORS

Ian Davies is a writer, teacher, music producer, and compulsive guitarist with a passion to share his love of the instrument in as simple, fun, and rewarding a way as possible. With over 30 years of teaching experience, Ian has helped thousands of beginners pick up the guitar and never put it down again!

His Guitar Mastery for Beginners series is designed to take new players on a step-by-step journey, using visuals, exercises, and easy-to-follow methods to ensure that they learn in the most effective, efficient, and enjoyable way possible.

When he's not writing, teaching, or playing concerts, Ian can usually be found deep in a jungle somewhere looking for birds.

*****

Paul Sterling is a guitarist, teacher, and writer who believes learning music should be enjoyable and rewarding. With years of experience helping beginners pick up the guitar, Paul has developed a clear, approachable style that turns challenges into breakthroughs.

His Guitar Mastery for Beginners series takes beginners on a step by step journey, making learning both practical and enjoyable.

When not teaching or writing, Paul can be found exploring new music, jamming with friends, or sharing his love for guitar with anyone eager to learn.

playfirstnote.com

ALSO BY First Note™

Beginner to Boss

OTHER BOOKS YOU MIGHT LIKE

GUITAR FRETBOARD MASTERY
FOR BEGINNERS

GUITAR TABS MASTERY
FOR BEGINNERS

NOTEBOOKS YOU MIGHT BE INTERESTED IN

GUITARIST'S ALL-IN-ONE PRACTICE NOTEBOOK

GUITAR SONGWRITER'S NOTEBOOK: TABS & CHORDS

Check all our books at

playfirstnote.com/books

Printed at Repro India Ltd.